Let There Be Light

The Seven Keys

BY THE SAME AUTHOR:

The Ancient Aramaic Prayer of Jesus

The Mysteries of Creation

LET THERE BE LIGHT

The Seven Keys

Rocco A. Errico

Devorss & Company
P.O. Box 550, Marina del Rey, CA. 90294-0550

Second Printing, 1987

ISBN: 0-87516-555-9
Library of Congress
Card Catalog Number: 85-71357

Printed in the United States of America

In gratitude
to
Mrs. Katherine W. Procter

CONTENTS

A Word from the Author

I was very fortunate to have had as my mentor and friend for ten years, the late Dr. George M. Lamsa, a native Assyrian, Near Eastern theologian, Aramaic expert, Bible translator, and ethnologist. In 1957 Dr. Lamsa completed and published his translation of the Holy Bible from Aramaic manuscripts.

In August 1962 I began a thorough study of all the published works of this great Eastern scholar and initiated classes based on the Aramaic perspective and unchanged Eastern customs. I then started to receive many requests from various denominations for a concise teaching system that presented the Bible through Eastern eyes. As a result of these requests, I developed the SEVEN KEYS. In the early 70's, after having been privately tutored for seven years by Dr. Lamsa, I extended this program throughout the United States.

My SEVEN KEYS course of study provides a broader understanding of the Bible whereby the teaching is not restricted by literal interpretations. This approach also makes it easier for those who have no previous knowledge of the Bible to grasp its meaning more readily. Since the very first presentation of the SEVEN KEYS, I have been inundated with letters requesting that the seminar material and additional information be published in book form. Hence, the birth of the present work: *LET THERE BE LIGHT—The Seven Keys.*

This book is based not only on my studies with Dr. Lamsa but also on my continued biblical research and more extensive knowledge of the Semitic languages of Aramaic and Hebrew. This approach is not based on any present school of biblical and textual criticism. The material is derived from the SEVEN KEYS seminar along with new information. It is a simple, direct approach using popular, everyday language and not weighty theological terminology. Its purpose is to familiarize the reader with the Semitic customs and thinking of the people among whom the Bible was born and to build a bridge into the world of the ancient Near East. It is not the intention of this work to convert the reader to a particular system of belief or interpretative viewpoint of the Bible. But rather, its purpose is to point to an alternate route one may take in searching and studying the Bible.

The majority of Scriptural quotations are from the King James Version of the Bible and are noted by the abbreviation KJV following each quote. I have also made use of the *Holy Bible from Ancient Eastern Manuscripts* and each quotation is identified as the Lamsa Translation. In the Scriptural quotations noted as the Aramaic Text, I have translated directly from the Aramaic-Peshitta Manuscripts: Ambrosianus Codex and the Mortimer-Macauley scrolls of the New Testament. All quotes from other authors may be found in the Reference Notes. This book should not be considered an exhaustive treatise but a beginner's panoramic view of the Bible through Eastern eyes.

LET THERE BE LIGHT—The Seven Keys is structured in two parts with an Introduction: Part One, Chapters 1-7, develops each of the SEVEN KEYS relating biblical examples; Part Two, Chapters 8-9, is a commentary on both the Old and New Testament verses chosen at random. The comments illustrate the application of the SEVEN KEYS to various passages of Scripture.

Above all, I sincerely hope you enjoy this book and find that its material will aid you in unlocking the door to almost four thousand years of antiquity and guide you into further enlightenment of the Scriptures. I have attempted as much as possible to avoid a collision with denominational interpretations of the Bible, but in certain passages of the Bible cited in this volume it became unavoidable. Apparently some Bible interpreters have unwittingly built monumental dogmas and confusing doctrines on a Bible verse that was only an idiom, metaphor, or custom.

I wish to express my sincere appreciation and thanks to Mr. and Mrs. George Smiley, Mr. and Mrs. Joseph T. Seem, and to the staff of the Noohra Foundation whose help made this book possible. Many thanks to Rev. Richard L. Hill, Vice President, for reading my manuscript many times and for his suggestions and positive input; Ms. Sue Edwards who proofread the material; Rev. Ann Milbourn, Administrator, for her support and assistance; Mrs. Jean Quirk for her labor of love in the hours spent typing and retyping this manuscript; and to the eternal Spirit who guides us all and who has brought this book into existence.

Introduction

We are about to embark on a great adventure. The path we will take is an unusual journey into the mysterious and often elusive world of the Near East. As we travel through the pages of the Holy Bible, we shall unlock many mysteries of the Book of Books that have appeared to be sealed for so many readers of the Scriptures. By the application of seven major keys to the various passages of the Bible we shall gain access to the uncomplicated spirit of the Book.

The seven keys enable the reader to perceive the beauty and creative force of the Bible as seen through Eastern eyes, thus learning to think and feel like the authors who were inspired by the Living Word which came to them. The motives and teachings of the Hebrew patriarchs, prophets, Jesus, and his apostles come alive through the use of the seven keys. As much as possible, I have avoided theological implications and interpretations of the Bible.

The purpose of this book is to clarify obscure passages of Scripture and any concepts of God, man, and the universe which we may have incorrectly understood from the biblical writers. By understanding the Bible from an Eastern perspective, we shall see more clearly an authentic and wholesome "image" of ourselves. The seven keys bridge almost four thousand years of antiquity. The seven keys are:

1. The Aramaic Language

2. The Idioms in the Bible

3. The Mysticism of the Near East

THE NUMBER SEVEN

Eastern people believe that numbers have more meaning than just their numerical value. They believe that the number seven is the most sacred of all numbers. An easterner usually uses the number seven in his everyday conversation. The biblical authors used the sacred number seven even more frequently in their writings. Some Bible authorities claim that the adoption of the number may have come from the ancient belief that there were seven planets which dominated the heavens: the sun, moon, Mercury, Venus, Mars, Jupiter, and Saturn. Be that as it may, according to the people of the East, seven signifies completeness and perfection. For this reason, we also use seven keys in our approach to the Scriptures.

THE SEMITIC BACKGROUND

It is very important to know the Eastern setting in which the Bible originated. We often forget that the sacred literature itself is an Eastern book. The majority of its teaching was written to Semitic peoples. The Holy Bible, with its spiritual and philosophical truths, has entered the Western world clothed in Near Eastern garments. This fact in itself presents a challenge for the Bible reader.

The late Dr. Abraham Rihbany, a Lebanese minister and author, puts this idea very succinctly in his book, *The Syrian Christ*:

The need of the Western readers of the Bible is, in my judgment, to enter sympathetically and intelligently into the atmosphere in which the books of the Scriptures first took form: to have real intellectual, as well as spiritual, fellowship with those Easterners who sought earnestly in their own way to give tangible form to those great spiritual truths which have been, and ever shall be, humanity's most precious heritage.[1]

We must always keep in mind the fact that the Scriptures were not written *to* us in the Western world, but that they were written *to* Eastern people. But the eternal truths which these Eastern biblical writers taught are applicable for all humanity. The following paragraphs outline a brief idea of each key and how the keys unlock the so-called "mysteries" of the Bible.

The First Key—Aramaic

In 1943 the Roman Catholic encyclical issued by the Pope stressed the need for interpreting the Scriptures to apply their lessons to then present conditions. The encyclical emphasized the importance of studying the biblical languages of Aramaic and Hebrew as *a sound basis for understanding the Scriptures*. Aramaic was the tongue spoken by Jesus Christ. And in 1971, the Roman Catholic Faith placed greater emphasis on the Bible.

The Vatican Ecumenical Council put the Bible in a place of prime importance in the Church. No longer do Roman Catholic biblical experts treat it as though it were factual in every detail. Like their Protestant colleagues, they are investigating the possibility that the Bible expresses ideas rather than clear-cut history. They are digging into Hebrew and

Aramaic texts. They are *searching for meanings perhaps still hidden.*[2]

Aramaic, Hebrew, and Greek are the three major languages most commonly used in biblical research and translations. In this approach, I have chosen the Aramaic langauage. Aramaic and Hebrew are cognate (sister) languages. In the very ancient days, Aramaic, a Semitic tongue, was the language of three powerful imperial nations: Assyria, Babylonia, and Persia (known today as Iran). Aramaic was also the spoken tongue of Palestine during the life of Jesus, and it remained the language of commerce and religion throughout the entire Near East until the 7th century, A.D. Then Arabic replaced Aramaic as the lingua franca of the Near East.[3]

Aramaic is far from being a dead language. To this very day, Aramaic is spoken in various parts of the world. There are many Assyrian Aramaic-speaking communities, large and small, throughout the United States, Lebanon, Iraq, Iran, Sweden, and Australia.

Jesus, his apostles, and contemporaries taught and preached in the Aramaic language. Papias (c. 60–130), Bishop of Hierapolis in Asia Minor, tells us that the gospel of Matthew was written in the Hebrew language, i.e., Aramaic. Reverend Carl Sumner Knoph, Ph.D., Dean of the School of Religion and Professor of Biblical Literature and Archaeology at the University of Southern California, states, "Sections of Matthew's gospel point quite definitely to a Greek rendering of a previous Aramaic original. . . ." (p. 33, Comrades of the Way—The Methodist Book Concern). Dr. Knoph also stated that Jesus and his disciples used the Jewish vernacular—Aramaic.

There is a theory promoted by some Western scholars that the remaining three gospels, Mark, Luke, and John, and also the book of Acts, were originally written in Aramaic.[4] Interestingly, there are a few biblical authorities in the East who claim that the *entire* New Testament was written in Aramaic before it was written in Greek. They believe that the New Testament was written in Palestinian Aramaic first; then translated into Greek, and later into the present Eastern Aramaic (Estrangela) from Greek. Be that as it may, it is not the intention of this book to defend or to prove Aramaic as the original source. My purpose is to focus on the Semitic, Aramaic tongue, its influence and importance in New Testament studies, English translations of biblical Aramaic texts, and the Near Eastern culture so that we may expand our understanding of the Bible from these Eastern perspectives.

In the coming chapters, we will apply the first key by showing some comparative differences between the King James Version of the Bible and English translations from Aramaic texts.

THE SECOND KEY—IDIOMS

The Bible is filled with idiomatic phrases. Idioms in any language have at one time or another caused misunderstanding. The Bible is no exception for there are many idiomatic sayings in the Scriptures that are not easy to comprehend simply because they are translated literally.

The definition of an idiom, along with many Scriptural idiomatic examples, will be explained in Chapter 2—Idioms in the Bible. However, the objective of this book is to acquaint the reader with various major ones.

THE THIRD KEY—MYSTICISM

We would be doing an injustice to Eastern people if we failed to recognize their mystical nature and capacity for spiritual dreams and visions. The mysticism of the Bible is always very practical. We must realize that the spiritual principles, and the mystical atmosphere of those principles themselves, have come from the very heart and soul of a living people. Easterners often say, "Our senses are capable of hearing the intimate whisperings of the divine Spirit."

Over forty percent of the Bible is based on mysticism. The spectrum of mysticism encompasses dreams, visions, voices, healings, clairaudience (inner hearing), clairvoyance (inner sight), and bi-location (out of body experiences). In the coming chapters, we will examine many passages of Scripture that deal with these mystical experiences.

THE FOURTH KEY—CULTURE

It is necessary to know more than just the geography of a country if we desire to understand the people of that country. Therefore, in order to flow with the spirit of the Bible, we must be familiar with the culture of the people. The biblical writers were greatly influenced by their own culture. The social habits, customs, and manners play an important role in the life of a nation. By studying the social forces that governed the inhabitants of the biblical lands, we shall be able to see the inner impulses that guided the authors of the Bible.

What makes our approach to the Eastern culture somewhat different than any other biblical system of study is this: In the mountain fastnesses of what is known today as Kurdistan, the discovery of a race of people, thought to be extinct, took place around the middle of the 19th century. This surviving remnant was descended from a nation that once ruled the ancient Near East, known as the Assyrians. These descendants, largely mixed with the blood of the ten Northern tribes of the House of Israel, still live, think, and speak as did the people among whom Jesus was born and to whom he taught his message. Here is a vital quote from a

British scholar who lived among these people, the late Dr. W. A. Wigram:

> We have now traced the history of a strange nation, from very early days to what is practically our own time—up to, in fact, the eve of the Great War . . . A strange survival in an isolated corner of the world, these last representatives of the ancient Assyrian stock have hitherto *kept up the most primitive of Semitic customs to an extent that can hardly be paralleled elsewhere,* even in Mesopotamian marsh districts. One thing is certain, that the Assyrians boast with justice that they ALONE of all Christian nations still keep as their spoken language what is acknowledged to be the language of Palestine in the first century, and that therefore they alone among Christian nations, if we except a few villages that may still exist in Lebanon, use regularly the language of Christ.[5]

THE FIFTH KEY—PSYCHOLOGY

Customs and psychology are bound together. Customs come from the psychological makeup of a nation. Easterners think differently than we do and therefore react to life's circumstances accordingly. For example, if you were an Easterner and wished to become a popular speaker, you would "play hard to get." In other words, you don't advertise yourself; you let people seek you out. Jesus said, "He who exalts himself shall be abased, and he who abases himself shall be exalted."

If you wished to congratulate a speaker, you would tell him, "I didn't understand a word you said." He would then look towards heaven and give many thanks to God. The inference is that the speaker was very deep and knowledgeable and that you as a listener would have to keep returning to hear him over and over again. You have actually paid him a compliment.

THE SIXTH KEY—SYMBOLISM

The symbolism of the Near East includes parables, poetical philosophy, and figurative speech. The Hebrew prophets made use of many symbols. For example, these seers often referred to imperial nations as lions, bears, and leopards and smaller powers as goats and lambs.

The book of Revelation contains over one thousand symbols. A symbol impresses the mind more quickly than mere words and is not so easily forgotten. For instance, the author of Revelation describes a lamb with seven horns and seven eyes, a description that would definitely make a lasting impression. Eastern people, of course, would be able to decipher the meaning almost immediately. The number seven represents perfection and completeness. The lamb signifies Jesus the Christ. The lamb also is symbolic of a Christ consciousness. The seven horns denote complete authority, and the seven eyes depict total vision and insight.

Parables are very important because Eastern teachers impart their ideas and concepts through stories. Once again, parables are told so that the listener will not forget the teaching. To an Easterner, a parable makes a greater impression than just statements of fact. Jesus, being an Easterner, taught his insights and imparted his teachings in parable form so that the masses would understand and remember his word. The prophets also used parables, allegories, and metaphors when they made their predictions.

The book of Job is the best example of poetical philosophy. The story of Job's successive calamities is a drama written in typical Eastern style to answer the philosophical question: Why do good people suffer? In the chapters that follow we will look deeply into the symbolism of the Bible.

THE SEVENTH KEY—AMPLIFICATION

Easterners enjoy putting more "color" into a situation rather than merely describing an actual happening with detailed accuracy. What better way is there to glorify an event and to make an everlasting impression than to amplify and magnify the occurrence! To help us see the idea of amplification, let us compare an event to a beautiful painting on canvas. When one frames a painting, the scene is then enhanced. The picture now has a setting. Thus Eastern people like to "frame" an event or situation. For instance, a speaker or writer will add more people, not in the hundreds but in the thousands, to his story. All this exaggerated expression of speech is done not to deceive, but to permanently frame an event and make it truly unforgettable.

CONCLUSION

We are about to begin our journey through the Scriptures using the "seven keys," unlocking many passages that have puzzled us, and shining light here and there. Whereever possible, we will by-pass doctrinal and denominational creeds and issues.

Now with the seven keys in our hands, we are ready to recline upon an imaginary flying carpet which will take us back into the ancient, mystical, biblical world of the Near East. Being carried by invisible airways, we shall travel through the pages of the Bible to discover clearer meanings in many events and episodes of this intriguing Book. Let us begin our adventure . . .

PART ONE

The Seven Keys

Chapters 1–7

CHAPTER 1

The First Key
Aramaic

ARAMAIC UNLOCKS THE DOOR

Before we begin applying the first key, the Aramaic language, it will be necessary to mention a few brief facts about Aramaic texts and something about the Aramaic-speaking people known as the Arameans.

Where and with whom does it all orginate? We must go back about four thousand years to a group of wandering desert people known as the Arameans. Somewhere in the northern section of the Arabian Desert, these wandering Aramean shepherds with their families belonged to the Semitic-language-speaking members of the white race. Later they came to be called Hebrews.[1]

In the New Standard Jewish Encyclopedia 1970, it clearly states the origin of the Hebrew patriarchs:

> According to the Bible (Gen. 10:22), Aram and Israel
> had a common ancestry and the Israelite patriarchs
> were of Aramaic origin and maintained ties of mar-
> riage with the tribes of Aram.[2]

Christianity and Islam have their roots in the teachings of the Hebrew patriarchs and prophets, which sprang from

3

a group of nomads known as the Arameans. The incredibly difficult desert life produced simplicity and equality among those Bedouins. To survive in the desert, these wandering tribal people felt a deep responsibility for other members of their clan. The outcome was a tight-knit family relationship and a strong sense of dignity and personal morality. The language these nomads spoke was an East Semitic dialect of Aramaic. The God that guided them in the vast, trackless deserts and uncharted lands of the Near East was known as the Provider.

Aramaic was the language of the Hebrew (Aramean) patriarchs. It was also the language of Jesus. The gospel was preached in the Aramaic tongue. The oldest complete Aramaic New Testament dates back to the sixth and seventh centuries A.D. The dates for the Aramaic texts of the Old Testament are disputed by scholars; some suggest the fifth century A.D. However, according to many of these biblical scholars, the Aramaic texts are reliable and often present clearer meanings to many obscure verses of the Bible.

BIBLICAL RIDDLES

As a minister and teacher of the Scriptures, I have been asked countless times about numerous obscure passages that keep people in the dark. There are hundreds of biblical verses that are difficult to understand and most readers find these verses bewildering. For instance, have you ever wondered why Jesus taught us to pray, *"lead us not into temptation?"* Does this imply that God may lead us into trouble? Is God ambivalent? In an August 1982 issue of *Newsweek*, there appeared an article entitled "Giving the Devil His Due," which suggests that God's nature is ambivalent. The religious writer cited the fact that Jesus taught his disciples to beseech the Father not to lead them into temptation. This, of course, confirmed for the author of the *Newsweek* article that Jesus' teaching affirmed God's ambivalence.[3]

And, have you ever been puzzled by the verse in Exodus which says, "For I the Lord thy God am a *jealous God?"* The apostle John says, "God is love." "Love" is a synonym for "God." But, is the infinite Presence which we call God really pure, unconditional love, or does God (Love) express jealousy? If so, of whom or of what is God jealous? Is the love of God limited by jealousy?

You may have questioned Jesus' words, "If any man come to me, and *hate not* his father, and mother, and wife, and children, and brethren, and sisters, yea, and his own life also, he cannot be my disciple." Is Jesus encouraging disobedience to the fifth commandment which decrees, "Honor your father and mother that your days may be long upon the land"? Matthew tells us that Jesus taught, "But I say unto you, love your enemies, and bless them that curse you, do good to them that hate you, and pray for them which despitefully use you, and persecute you." Jesus clearly teaches us to love our enemies, and yet for one to be his disciple one must apparently hate his parents and family. How do we reconcile this?

Have you also tried to figure out why God, the Father and Source of abundant mercies, would forsake and desert Jesus on the cross? After all, we are told that Jesus was obeying the Father's will by accepting the crucifixion. (See Matt. 26:39) Would God withhold his comforting presence when Jesus needed him most? What kind of loving father would abandon his own son at such a crucial hour of suffering? Yet we read in the New Testament that Jesus cried out, "My God, My God, why has thou forsaken me?"

You could, I am sure, add many more contradictory passages to the few I have suggested. I have seen some people, out of great frustration, completely turn aside from reading the Bible, feeling that so much of what they read denies a positive, universal, and relevant philosophy of life for them. The problem of trying to bridge almost 4,000 years of antiquity is too much, and in a manner of speaking, this is true for a large majority of people. On the other hand, there is also the dilemma of those who were taught to accept the puzzling biblical contradictions on faith alone.

The question is, can some of these difficulties be solved? The answer is YES! As we explore the various passages through English translations of Aramaic texts of the Bible, we will find clearer renditions of these verses and avoid wrestling with the old Scriptural contradictions of the past.

RIDDLES SOLVED

When Jesus said, "lead us not into temptation," he spoke the Aramaic words, *oola talan*, meaning, "And let us *not enter*." So what Jesus actually said was, "And let us not enter into temptation." Matt. 6:13, Lamsa translation. The meaning is clear. Jesus, through his prayer, teaches that our minds must remain alert so as not to be ensnared by an alluring trap. Benjamin Franklin also found our present English rendering of this verse undesirable and changed the verse to read, "and keep us out of temptation." Can you imagine! Benjamin Franklin sensed the meaning of the Aramaic words without knowing the language.

What about the problem of God's jealousy? The Aramaic term *tanana* means "zealous," "jealous," and "ardent desire." Therefore, a more appropriate translation of what God told Moses is "because I am the Lord your God, a zealous God." Ex. 20:5, Aramaic text. The word "zealous" denotes a divine care, whereas the term "jealous" implies that other gods did exist, and that the Lord God was in competition with and jealous of the other deities. However, this was not the situation. God was zealous for his people. Law, order, justice, and righteousness were to reign among the Hebrews. Then again in Exodus 34:14, the verse is rendered, "For thou shalt worship no other god; for the LORD, whose name is Jealous, is a jealous God." KJV. But the Aramaic text reads, "For you shall worship no other god; for the LORD, whose name is Zealous, is a zealous God." It is also interesting to note that the Hebrew word *kanna* may also be translated as zealous instead of jealous.

In November 1961, an article appearing in a Soviet scientific and religious publication deprecated Christianity and made reference to numerous "contradictory and hypocritical morals and teachings of Christian churches and theologies. . . ." Among the many objections the article raised was Jesus' command to "hate" one's family in order to be his disciple. This has confused many people in addition to the Russian writer, for even though we know Jesus' meaning was to put his teachings first above all else, we still have to contend with the word "hate" which remains in the Scriptural text.

A few years ago a syndicated religious column in our American newspapers answered the question of why Jesus chose the word "hate." The column stated that Jesus did not mean to "hate," but to "love less." The religious writer went on to explain the Aramaic meaning of the word. But, alas, the truth is that nowhere in any Aramaic dictionary does the word mean "to love less." Nor, for that matter, does the word even mean "to love *a little less.*"

Sna is a strong Aramaic word meaning "to hate," "to detest," and "to despise." In fact, the Aramaic term *sna* has five basic meanings: "to hate," "to stand up straight," "to put out the candle or light," "a threshing floor," and "to set to one side." Thus, by using the last meaning, we see that Jesus actually said, "He who comes to me and *does not put to one side* his father and his mother. . . ." Jesus knew that anyone who wished to be his disciple would be challenged by his or her family. His teaching contradicted much of the literal interpretation of the Scriptures and the teachings of the elders.

Jesus had warned the people about the consequences of his teachings. "Think not that I am come to send peace on earth: I come not to send peace, but a sword. For I am come to set a man at variance against his father and the daughter against her mother, and the daughter-in-law against her mother-in-law." Matt. 10:34–35, KJV. The term "sword" is used as a metaphor in the Aramaic language and means "division." When a member of a strict orthodox family of Judaism would embrace the teachings of Jesus, other members of the family would ostracize him or her. Some of them would even be delivered into the hands of the authorities to receive severe punishment or death. Hence the meaning of Jesus' statement, "And a man's foes shall be they of his own household." Now we can understand what Jesus intended when he said, "He who comes to me and does not put to one side his father and his mother, . . . cannot be my disciple." We can also see that being less loving had nothing to do with what Jesus said or meant.

There is an utterance which Jesus made from the cross that has been a serious stumbling block for many sincere students of the Bible. "And about the ninth hour," reports the writer of the gospel, "Jesus cried with a loud voice, saying *Eli, Eli, l'mana sabachthani?* That is to say, My God, my God, why hast thou forsaken me?" Matt. 27:46, KJV. All Greek texts of the Bible have retained this statement of Jesus in Aramaic.

I have written a transliteration of these Aramaic words, followed by a literal translation. Notice that the King James Version of the Bible represents Jesus' utterance as having been a question, suggesting that Jesus did not understand what was happening and that he felt forsaken by God. But his actual words were a declaration, a statement: "*'EL, 'EL, L'MANA SHABAKTHANI:* Oh God! Oh God! To what (a purpose) You have kept me!" This is an exclamation of victory, as Jesus cries out with a deep knowingness of his reason for having lived and for dying. An even more literal rendering would be, "Oh Sustainer! Oh Sustainer! To what (a purpose) You have left me!" Being "left" as it is used here does not mean "forsaken" or "abandoned," but means "remaining to fulfill an end or destiny." In the Lamsa translation of the Bible, the verse is translated as, "And about the ninth hour, Jesus cried out with a loud voice and said, *ELI, ELI, LEMANA SHABAKTHANI*: My God, my God, for this I was spared!" or "This was my destiny!"

THE TWENTY-SECOND PSALM

Some biblical authorities claim that Jesus was quoting the 22nd Psalm which reads, "My God, my God, why hast thou forsaken me? Why art thou so far from helping me, and from the words of my roaring?" KJV. Dr. George Lamsa suggests that Jesus was not quoting the 22nd Psalm during his suffering on the cross. In his translation of the Peshitta, Aramaic text, verse one of this psalm is translated, "My God, my God, why has thou let me to live? and yet thou hast delayed my salvation from me, because of the words of my folly." In an article entitled "Introduction to the Psalms," Dr. Lamsa, makes the following remarks:

The Aramaic word *SHABAKTHANI* which appears in Psalm 22 is rendered "let me live," that is, "spare me" instead of "forsaken me." Easterners when suffering in distress wonder why they live and ask God why he has spared them, and why he has not taken them like their fathers. The phrase *L'MANA SHABAKTHANI* is also used by Easterners to confirm one's destiny (See Matt. 27:46, Lamsa translation).

SHABAK also means "to keep" as in Rom. 11:4, Isa. 10:3, Isa. 14:1 of the Eastern text and "to forgive" as in Matt. 6:12. It can also be translated "forsake" with the sense of sparing, that is, letting a person live but doing nothing to relieve his suffering.

God forsakes no one. He is mindful of all his children. Nevertheless, sometimes when we are discouraged or suffering, we wonder why our deliverance is delayed and why God does not act promptly. God is patient and does things in his own way. In Psalm 22, the psalmist wonders why he or Israel has been spared to go through so many struggles, and why God has not speedily punished their enemies. At the same time he is mindful of God's presence as he converses with him. If God had forsaken him, how could the psalmist converse with him?[4]

Not anywhere does the Aramaic text of the New Testament suggest that Jesus was asking a question or expressing doubt. Instead, when the original Aramaic intent is correctly understood, it strongly affirms that Jesus was fully aware of his Father's presence and closeness throughout his entire crucifixion. The cross was a victory over death and revealed to humanity the meaning of immortality. Jesus, through his resurrection, abolished the fear of death and opened for us a new understanding of life eternal. The apostle Paul, in his letter to Timothy, encourages the young minister with these words, "For God has not given us the spirit of fear, but of power and of love and of good discipline. . . . And is now made manifest by the appearing of our Savior Jesus Christ, *who has abolished death and has revealed life and immortality* through the gospel." 2 Tim. 1:7, 10, Aramaic text.

AN ANCIENT COMMENTARY

There is an ancient commentary on this very utterance of Jesus from the cross written in the 9th century. The title of the scroll reads, "The Testimony (Evidence) from the Book of Commentaries of Lord Ishodad of Merv, Bishop of Hadatha, Beth Naharain (Mesopotamia) 850 A.D. Bishop of the Church of the East." Unfortunately, this intriguing and illuminating commentary is available only in the Aramaic language. However, I have translated a small portion of it here. The English rendering appears somewhat clumsy because I want to retain the force and intent of the writer; also as much as possible, I give a word-for-word translation, retaining its original style of punctuation. The Commentary is as follows:

> The explanation of *'EL, 'EL, L'MANA SHABAK-TANI: Not at all was he forsaken by the Godhead.* Not even during suffering nor during death because *the Godhead was always with him*—in suffering and on the cross and in death and in the grave; And very God Himself raised him in power and in glory as in the psalm of David: 'For You have not left my soul in *SHEOL*: And neither have You allowed Your holy one to see corruption.'[5]

(According to ancient Hebrew belief, *SHEOL* is a place of silence and inactivity for the departed soul.) This comment by Ishodad is a reassuring testimony to the comforting power and presence of God.

The lesson we learn is that God is always with us, in suffering as well as in joy. The fact is God never forsakes any of us at any time, anywhere! His truth, power and presence are ever working to guide all humanity into paths of enlightenment.

COMPARATIVE DIFFERENCES

There is a proverb which says, ''The proof of the pudding is in the eating.'' Here are some varied differences based on Aramaic texts, as compared to the King James Version of the Bible. The direct translations from Aramaic verses to English shed much light upon these passages, and with some of them the meaning changes completely. In this section of comparative texts, I make no comments on the verses but allow the reader to evaluate the differences:

Genesis 1:1

In the beginning God created the heaven and the earth. (KJV)

God (Alaha) created the essence heaven and the essence earth in the very beginning. (Aramaic)

Job 12:6

The tabernacles of robbers prosper, and they that provoke God are secure; into whose hand God bringeth abundantly. (KJV)

The tents of robbers shall perish, and the assurance of those who incite God because there is no God in their hearts. (Aramaic)

Job 31:10

Then let my wife grind unto another, and let others bow down upon her. (KJV)

Then let my wife grind (meal) for others and let her bake bread at another man's place. (Aramaic)

Psalm 7:11

God judgeth the righteous, and God is angry with the wicked every day. (KJV)

God (Alaha) is a just judge and He is not angry every day. (Aramaic)

Psalm 23:2

He maketh me to lie down in green pastures; he
leadeth me beside the still waters.   (KJV)

And he makes me dwell in pastures of strength. He
guides me by refreshing waters.   (Aramaic)

Psalm 23:6

Surely goodness and mercy shall follow me all the
days of my life; and I will dwell in the house of the
Lord forever.   (KJV)

Your loving kindness and compassions have pur-
sued me all the days of my life; and I shall live in the
house of the Lord for the length of days.   (Aramaic)

Psalm 46:10

Be still and know that I am God!   (KJV)

Return to me and know that I am God!   (Aramaic)

Isaiah 43:28

Therefore I have profaned the princes of the sanctuary, have given Jacob to the curse and Israel to re-
proaches.   (KJV)

Your princes have defiled the holy place (the sanctuary); therefore I have given Jacob to the curse and
Israel to shame.*   (Aramaic)

Jeremiah 4:10

Then said I, Ah Lord God; surely thou hast greatly
deceived this people and Jerusalem, saying, Ye shall

---

*The Septuagint, Greek text of the Old Testament, agrees with
the Peshitta, Aramaic text on Isa. 43:28. Isaiah states that the
noblemen or chiefs of the people had defiled the sanctuary. According to the KJV, Isaiah claims that the Lord God defiled the
princes. (To defile means to commit impure acts.)

have peace; whereas the sword reacheth unto the soul. (KJV)

Then I said, I implore you, Oh Lord God, truly, I have deceived this people and Jerusalem exceedingly because I have said, You will have peace, and behold, the slaying sword reaches as far as the soul. (Aramaic)

Matthew 5:3

Blessed are the poor in spirit; for theirs is the kingdom of heaven. (KJV)

Blessed are the gentle, for theirs is the kingdom of heaven. (Aramaic)

Matthew 6:34

Take therefore no thought for the morrow; for the morrow shall take thought for things of itself. Sufficient unto the day is the evil thereof. (KJV)

Now do not be anxious about the future; for the future will take care of itself. Enough for the day are its own problems. (Aramaic)

2 Timothy 3:16

All scripture is given by inspiration of God and is profitable for doctrine, for reproof, for correction, for instruction in righteousness. (KJV)

All scripture that is written by the Spirit is useful for teaching, correction, right action, and for instruction in justice. (Aramaic)

2 Peter 1:21

For the prophecy came not in old time by the will of man but holy men of God spoke as they were moved by the Holy Ghost. (KJV)

For prophecy at no time ever came by the will of man, but holy men of God spoke when they were impelled by the Holy Spirit. (Aramaic)

1 Corinthians 7:18

Is any man called being circumcised? Let him not become uncircumcised. (KJV)

If any man were circumcised when he was called, let him not turn to the party of the uncircumcised.

(Aramaic)

There are literally thousands of "variants" in comparative scriptural passages, and a special volume would have to be written to cover all of them. We have applied the first key, the Aramaic language, to just a few verses of the Bible, and we can see how enlightening the Aramaic text actually is.

For those readers who wish to pursue the translation in other areas of the Bible, I suggest *THE HOLY BIBLE*, from *Ancient Eastern Manuscripts*, by George M. Lamsa, Th.D. This translation is based solely on Aramaic manuscripts from Genesis to Revelation. Dr. Lamsa claims there are approximately 10,000 to 12,000 differences.

Besides translation differences, there is another fascinating avenue to be explored from the language of Jesus, and that avenue is the idiomatic expressions. There are many more puzzling episodes ready to be clarified by applying the second key—Idioms.

CHAPTER 2

The Second Key
Idioms

COLLOQUIALISMS

First of all, what is an idiom? An idiom is a peculiar expression of speech which says one thing but means something else. All languages have their own set of unusual expressions of speech, and it becomes necessary for anyone who is learning a new language to become familiar with the peculiar colloquialisms. For instance, if one were to learn Spanish, he would have to know that "Estoy bruja," does not mean "I am a witch" but rather "I have no money." The words "Estoy bruja," literally translate as "I am a witch."

I am sure you have at one time or another either used or heard these American idioms: "I'm going to hit the sack (or the hay)," or "I'm going to sack out." Have you ever known anyone who has been in "hot water" for weeks and months on end? Or perhaps he was "up in the air" for several days over a business deal. We "blow our tops," "lose our marbles," and "become hot under the collar." Have you or a friend ever been "in a pickle" or "in a jam?" Have you ever paid "an arm and a leg" for some item? Some of us dress "fit to kill." We put "bugs in people's ears" and ask them to "get off our backs." Sometimes we even go around with a "chip on our shoulder," and we want to "get it straight from the horse's mouth." We also know people who "stew around" or "drop in the office." Some business men and women remain "chained to their desks" all day long.

Many immigrants coming to the United States have difficulty understanding us when we speak English; and many are the foreign scholars whose use of English is impeccable, yet they are lost in the maze of everyday, common speech when they arrive on our shores. How would they understand that Mickey Mantle "died on third base," or that the "Redskins scalped the Cowboys?" Our sports jargon can be ridiculously funny if taken literally.

The fact is that we carry on conversations most of the time using idiomatic expressions and we don't even stop to think about them. Try to "catch yourself" during the day every time you use an English idiom. You'll be surprised at how often you say one thing but mean something else.

I can remember as a child listening to one of my favorite radio programs, LIFE WITH LUIGI. The entire format of this half hour program was built on idioms. The "gags" were very funny because Luigi would often take an American idiom literally. He was an Italian immigrant who spoke "broken" English. I recall a radio episode which illustrates how literally he took English phrases of speech: Luigi had just received his driver's license, and while driving home he decided to make a "U" turn where it was forbidden to do so. An officer saw the poor man make the turn, chased him down, brought him back to the sign, and questioned him about his ability to read. Luigi replied, "I can read." The officer then asked him to read the street sign. The nervous Italian began to read, "It's-a-say, *No U Turn.*" The patrolman questioned, "Do you know what that means?" Luigi quickly and happily answered, "Yes, no *You-A-Turn* means it's-a-*My Turn.*" Interestingly, we have been exactly like Luigi while reading the Bible. We mistakenly took the biblical idioms literally. There are over a thousand idioms in the Bible. They were translated faithfully and accurately—but literally; therefore their actual meanings are misconstrued.

BIBLICAL IDIOMS

Let's examine at random a few of these idioms from the Scriptures. God said to Adam, "Cursed is the ground for thy sake; *thorns* and *thistles* shall it bring forth to thee . . . in the *sweat of thy face* shalt thou eat bread, till thou return to the ground." Gen. 3:18–19, KJV. It reads as though God created thorns, thistles, and perspiration specifically to punish man, although our common sense tells us something else. We know that thorns and thistles are nature's way of protecting certain species of plants, and that perspiring is how the body cools itself when overheated, and that it is also a means of releasing toxins. None of these things is a "curse." But to us thorns and thistles are irksome and can be painful. Hence, the idiom means that existence for Adam would become burdensome because he had departed from a clear understanding of life. And "sweat," in the figurative style of the Near East, refers idiomatically to the hardship which man's false philosophical outlook on life brings upon him. In actuality, God never cursed man, woman, or the earth. Man, himself, through ignorance and acting out his own self-defeating thought patterns, encounters "thorns" and "thistles," and eats bread in the "sweat of his face." However, the biblical text definitely states that God cursed the man, woman, serpent, and the earth. But we must understand that this narrative is a parable and it should not be taken as a literal event. (See Chapter 6, SYMBOLISM, Adam and Eve).

Another interesting idiom is that of Lot's wife turning into a "pillar of salt." Actually this means she suffered a stroke, became paralyzed and died.[1]

Here is an additional example. While on his deathbed, the Hebrew patriarch Jacob (whose name later was changed to Israel) called his twelve sons before him. He blessed each of them and prophesied to them concerning themselves and their future generations. According to the Eastern custom, the aged patriarch would lift his head toward heaven, and with outstretched hands, say, "Gather yourselves together and hear, O sons of Jacob; and listen to Israel your father. . . ." Gen. 49.2, Aramaic text. The wise father turned first to Reuben and prophesied to him, then to Simeon and Levi. Then to Judah, he said, "he washed his garments in wine, and his clothes in the blood of grapes; his eyes shall be red with wine, and his teeth white with milk." Gen. 49:11–12, KJV. Israel blessed his son, Judah, with great prosperity. To "wash garments with wine and blood (juice) of the grape" and to "have eyes red from wine" means Judah would have many prolific vineyards— he would prosper abundantly. He would also own many flocks of goats and sheep, thus having more than ample milk— great prosperity and success through vineyards and livestock.[2] Obviously, then, we should not attempt to take any of these statements absolutely literally.

Today, in the Near East, the rug sellers and merchants of any fine crafts or clothing bargain with prospective buyers in the traditional Eastern manner. Their language is very colorful, and of course the names of God and all His holy angels, saints, prophets, and apostles are brought into the conversation while bartering. To make an impression, the seller will say, "In the most precious name of Allah (God) this rug was done by His hand," or "the finger of Allah made this garment." What the merchant means is "the rug is perfect" and "the garment is flawless." To have the hand or finger of God involved in anything is a beautiful way of saying, "This is the finest craftsmanship in the world."

The rug, garment, or other merchandise is equated with God to show absolute perfection, ultimate beauty, and excellence.

And so we read in the Scriptures that when God "finished talking with him on the mountain of Sinai, He gave to Moses two tablets of testimony, tablets of stone that were written by the finger of Alaha." Ex. 31:18, Aramaic text. The witness in stone was the Law, i.e., The Ten Commandments written by "the finger of God." Moses had been tutored by the finest magicians in Egypt. He had studied the wisdom and esoteric teachings of the Assyrians, the Babylonians, and the Egyptians. He was familiar with the Code of Hammurabi, the Lawgiver of Babylon, and he knew Egyptian civil law. So, for Moses to come down from the mountain with only ten commandments, and not one hundred, was truly a revelation from God. The Law was perfect, flawless, sure; hence, "done by God's finger."

POETIC IDIOMS

The poetical language of the Bible has always been enchanting, but here again we find idiomatic colloquialisms which can be confusing if taken literally. Who can forget the admonition to youth in the book of Ecclesiastes: (The colloquial expressions are explained in the parentheses)

Remember now thy Creator in the days of thy youth, while the evil days come not, nor the years draw nigh, when thou shalt say, I have no pleasure in them; . . . In the days when the keepers of the house shall tremble (legs begin to tremble), and the strong men shall bow themselves (the arms lose their strength), and the grinders cease because they are few (loss of teeth and the ability to chew), and those that look out the windows be darkened (eyesight grows dim). And the doors shall be shut in the streets, when the sound of the grinding is low, (ears become so hard of hearing that the sound of women grinding at the mill is low). And he shall rise up at the voice of the bird, and all the daughters of musick shall be brought low; (difficulty in distinguishing sounds and being disturbed by the song of birds) . . . And the almond tree shall flourish, and the grasshopper shall be a burden [Aramaic text reads . . . "and the locust shall multiply,"] (your children will multiply quickly and you'll see your grandchildren and great grandchildren). Or ever the silver cord be loosed, (before passions fade and life draws to a close) or the golden bowl be broken, or the pitcher be broken at the fountain, or the wheel broken at the cistern. (before life comes to an end, or before the loss of sexual potency and virility)[3] Ecc. 12:1-6, KJV.

It is clear that not only incorrect translations may have contributed to a misunderstanding of the Bible, but also correct and literal translations may have created an equally difficult problem for readers who did not allow for colorful idiomatic usages.

The Hebrew prophets provided more good examples of idiomatic usage. These men were statesmen who dearly loved their own nation, Israel, but were concerned about the welfare of other nations as well. The task of pointing out the evils of their own people and government was quite a difficult one, and to accomplish this they made their revelations very graphic and impressive. Their style was terse, direct, and intense, with ideas skillfully couched in descriptive metaphors and idiomatic terms.

These wise, ancient sages wanted the Hebrew people, not just their government officials, to understand their ideas and messages, and to accomplish this they used the common vernacular of everyday expressions. Because of their colloquial method of speaking and writing, the prophets were highly successful in conveying messages clearly to the common people of the Near East, although the Western reader has a problem understanding this purely Eastern style of speech. Because of the frequent use of symbolism, a style of communication not often employed in the West, and the use of the vernacular and idioms peculiar to Eastern people, the Western mind is at a loss to interpret the prophecies clearly. And not only ordinary readers, but many Bible authorities take the symbols too literally, resulting in various schools of interpretation.

PROPHETIC IDIOMS

What were some of the idiomatic terms employed by the prophets? The following quotation from Isaiah illustrates several idioms with the intended meaning included in the parentheses:

> For the day of the Lord of hosts shall be upon everyone that is proud and lofty . . . upon all the cedars of Lebanon. . . and upon the oaks of Bashan (great, noble, strong, proud, influential men) . . . and upon all the hills that are lifted up (smaller powers that have exalted themselves).[4] Isa. 2:12–14, KJV.

Again, this great statesman speaks idiomatically: "Cease ye from man whose breath is in his nostrils; for wherein is he to be accounted of?" Isa. 2:22, KJV. But how does one avoid a man "whose breath is in his nostrils?" We would have to avoid everyone if we were to take the prophet's word literally. However, this idiom really means "stay away from the man who is continually angry, explosive, and impulsive" . . . which certainly is a very good piece of advice.

In this famous and often quoted prophecy of Isaiah there

are numerous idioms which, unfortunately, have been interpreted in a literal sense.

> The wolf also shall dwell with the lamb, and the leopard shall lie down with the kid; and the calf and the young lion and the fatling (in Aramaic, ''ox'') together; and a little child shall lead them. And the cow and the bear shall feed together; their young ones shall lie down together; and the lion shall eat straw like an ox. (Aramaic, ''with the serpent'') and the weaned child shall put his hand on the cockatrice's den (Aramaic, ''asp's den''). Isa. 11:6–8, KJV.

Are we really to expect leadership from a small child? Will the animals of the earth actually undergo a change of nature? ''A little child shall lead them,'' for instance, indicates that political leadership will be in the hands of simple, sincere people rather than in the hands of the shrewd and doubledealing, who pervert justice and maintain double standards of law and order. And though ''a little child'' is open and trusting, the prophecy does not mean that a simpleton will hold office; rather, it will be a person of integrity with an inner understanding for all concerned. The ''suckling child playing with serpents'' and the ''weaned child putting his hand in the den of the asp'' symbolize the power of ''pure'' leaders to negotiate with their enemies (serpents and asps). It will take a sincere, persuasive person with a pure mind to be able to move his enemy toward favoring his nation instead of conquering it.

The prophets often used animals, especially the wild, vicious predators that frequently terrorized small towns, to symbolize strong, powerful, dictatorial nations. The ''wolf,'' ''leopard,'' ''lion,'' and ''bear'' indicate oppressive nations that seek to devour the helpless and defenseless nations. The ''lamb,'' ''kid,'' ''calf,'' and ''cow'' symbolize weaker and smaller nations. All of these animals, eating and dwelling together, and being led by a child, means that strong nations will be in harmony with the defenseless nations; they will trade and be at peace with one another. "The lion shall eat straw like an ox" is symbolic of the day when powerful nations will be content with their own internal resources and not seek to devour other nations by plundering them. Isaiah saw truth and justice pouring out to all nations as a result of the Messiah's power and teaching. The Messiah was to reveal the truth of God to all men everywhere so that peace and harmony would reign among the nations.

JESUS' USE OF IDIOMS

Jesus also made use of idiomatic expressions when he taught. Let us examine some of these expressions from the four "gospels" which in Aramaic are called the "preachings" of Matthew, Mark, Luke and John.

In Matthew 5:22, Jesus says: "but whoever shall say, Thou fool, shall be in danger of hell-fire." Can this really be so? Most of us at one time or another have referred to ourselves or others as "fools," and according to the majority of our English translations of the teachings of Jesus, this would be cause for condemnation to "hell-fire."

The Aramaic term which has been translated "fool" is LELA. This Aramaic word has no equivalent in modern English. LELA is a word no longer used by Aramaic-speaking people today. It was a culturally offensive term and implied a deeply insensitive, grossly brutish, uncouth person, a stupid, ignorant individual. It was definitely a defamatory remark that incited grave consequences—a trouble-making word which made the blood boil with anger, precipitated feuds, and brought "hell-fire."

The term *GAYHANA DNOORA*, "hell-fire," means "regret," and "mental torment." According to the Aramaic-speaking Church fathers of the 2nd to 5th centuries, A.D. "hell-fire" denoted torment of mind, *not* an inferno in which God burns people forever. Later on hell came to be known as a designated place of punishment for the wicked and unbelievers. But among the early Eastern Church fathers of Edessa and Nisibin, Mesopotamia, this doctrine was not prevalent.

HELL

What and where is "hell?" Some believe it is a subterranean torture pit in which living souls are burned in torment throughout eternity. Others teach that it is a place of unending separation from the presence of God. These fiery concepts of hell and punishment came from certain misunderstood passages of the Bible and from the interpretations of some of the early Church fathers such as Tertullian and Augustine. Hell is not a place where God tortures "disobedient" children. Such a meaning was never intended by Jesus when he used the Aramaic term, *GAYHANA DNOORA*.

Our English word "hell" is from the Anglo-Saxon *HEL*, "a hidden place," and it is derived from *HELAN*, and means "to hide." But that one word, *HEL*, was used by translators to render two separate Semitic terms—the Hebrew *SHEOL* and the Aramaic *GAYHANA DNOORA*—which have entirely different meanings.

The word *SHEOL* is derived from the Hebrew *SHALAL*, "to be still or quiet." In the ancient days, the Hebrews believed that sheol was a place below the surface of the earth where departed souls, both good and bad, remained quiet and inactive, awaiting the day of judgment. They also believed God had no jurisdiction over *SHEOL*.

The Aramaic, *GAYHANA* or *GAYHANA DNOORA* was used only in the New Testament, and mostly by Jesus, though at times, he did use the term *SHEOL*. *GAYHANA* means "Valley of Hinnom," which was a place outside Jerusalem where the people burned rubbish, and in the very ancient days, it was a place of sacrifice to the pagan Ammonite god, Molech. (See 2 Kings 23:10, and 2 Chron. 33:6, KJV) In the New Testament times, *GAYHANA* was used idiomatically to indicate "regret," "remorse," "mental agony," or "mental suffering." The term "hell" was understood in the East by the Aramaic-speaking early Church fathers, but it has been interpreted literally and misunderstood in the West.

Difficult Admonitions

Another well-known admonition is, "If thy right eye offend thee, pluck it out and cast it from thee, . . . and if thy right hand offend thee, cut it off, and cast it from thee." Matt. 5:29–30, KJV. Jesus' words occasionally seem to be harsh and unfeeling, and truly, if some of his words were taken literally, we'd be in a great deal of difficulty. For example, according to Jesus, if you commit an offense with your hand, you should cut it off. Not many people have taken these words literally, but from time to time, a few have actually gone so far as to cut off their hands in obedience to his teaching. In Iraq, and in many other Eastern countries where the law is very strictly upheld, those who are caught stealing have one hand cut off by the city officials; on the second offense, the remaining hand is lost; on the third offense, the head is removed. This greatly discourages stealing.

Jesus, however, was not teaching literally to cut off the hand, but rather to cut out, or cease, the habit of stealing. To "pluck out" or to "cut off" simply means to "quit it," to "stop it"—and "don't do it anymore."

Jesus told his apostles that certain signs would follow those who believe in his name. "And these signs shall follow them that believe; In my name . . . they shall take up serpents; and if they drink any deadly thing it shall not hurt them. . . .'' Mark 16:17–18, KJV. With these encouraging declarations, Jesus empowered his disciples "to take up serpents," that is, "to handle" fearlessly the challengers and enemies of his gospel. The illiterate followers of Jesus would be inspired by divine wisdom to answer religious leaders, cunning officials, and those who opposed his simple message. "Drinking poison" without harm refers to the power to overcome all the malicious gossip and false accusations made against the followers of Jesus. They were not to be afraid of being maligned, for they would "drink it," that is, withstand the onslaught of slander and not be hurt by it.

Jesus also taught his followers that they could "remove mountains," which means conquer severe obstacles and difficulties; "tread on serpents," which means conquer fear and override the power of their enemies; and "cast out devils," which means heal the mentally and emotionally ill. Jesus' teachings were so dynamic and uplifting to the consciousness of the apostles that they, too, manifested the same kind of physical, mental, and spiritual transforming power as their lord and teacher.

Paul's Use of Idioms

The apostle Paul, in his epistles, also made use of Aramaic idioms when he taught. In his letter to the Corinthians he says, "O ye Corinthians, our mouth is open to you, our heart is enlarged. Ye are not straitened in us, but ye are straitened in your own bowels." 2 Cor. 6:11–12, KJV. Let us compare a translation of this same verse from Aramaic. "Our mouths are open toward you, Corinthians, and our hearts breathe freely. You are not compelled by us but are strongly urged by your tender compassions." Still, we wonder, exactly what does all this mean?

The apostle writes frankly to the Corinthians when he

uses the idiom, "our mouths are open toward you," meaning "we have told you everything." In the Near East, when a man declares himself plainly and reveals all, it is said, "He has a big mouth." In English a person who can't keep a secret is said to have "a big mouth." The Aramaic does not have this negative connotation.

This same idiom is used in the Old Testament. 1 Samuel 2:1 reads, "And Hannah prayed, and she said . . . my mouth is enlarged over my enemies . . ." The Aramaic rendering is, "And Hannah prayed and said . . . my mouth is opened against my enemies." Here we have the identical idiom which the apostle Paul used, but in this case it conveys a different meaning.

Hannah had been deeply distressed for years because she had borne no children. For a married woman of the East to be childless is a horrible stigma, and because Hannah had been unable to conceive, she had been tormented and ridiculed by her husband's other wife, Pannah. No doubt, the women of the town gossiped about her, for the belief system of the Hebrews at that time was that any woman who has not been able to bear a child was in the disfavor of the Lord.

After receiving a spoken blessing from the High Priest Eli, Hannah gave birth to a son and named him Samuel. After the birth of Samuel, she had many more children, and now she cries, "My mouth is opened against my enemies," that is, "I am able to talk back to my tormentors who ridiculed me— God favors me—I've had a child." Thus, the Aramaic idiom, "open mouth," has two meanings: "to talk back to" and "to reveal everything."

The other unusual idiom which Paul used, "our hearts breathe freely," means "our conscience is clear" or "we are relieved." The last part of the verse is very interesting also, "ye are not straitened in us, but ye are straitened in your own bowels." The translation of the original word as "bowels" is not incorrect, but the meaning is lost because the Aramaic word in this verse is *RAKHMA* and has at least a dozen English equivalents. Literally the word means "friends,""bowels," "womb," "bladder," "testicles," and "the female sexual organs." The same word, *RAKHMA* used metaphorically, means "love," "mercy," "kindness," "affection," "compassion," "benevolence," "friendliness," and "tenderheartedness." In this instance, the intended meaning is actually "compassion."

Where else was this particular idiom or metaphor written in the Scriptures? In Philippians, Paul very tender-heartedly says, "For God is my record, how greatly I long after you all in the bowels of Jesus Christ." Phil. 1:8, KJV. The Aramaic text, however, reads, "Indeed Alaha (God) is my witness as to what manner I fiercely love all of you through the tender love of Jesus the Anointed One."

Isaiah, communing with the Lord God, prays, "Look down from heaven . . . Where is thy zeal and thy strength, the sounding of thy bowels and of thy mercies toward me? Are they restrained?" Isa. 63:15, KJV. The idiom "the sounding of bowels" means "tender affection and love." In Aramaic, this part of the verse reads, "turn your tender affections and love upon me." In another passage, the prophetic statesman declares, "Wherefore my bowels shall sound (talk) like an harp for Moab . . ." Isa. 16:11, KJV. "My heart shall sorrow over Moab," is the prophet's real meaning.[5]

Another idiom using the word "bowels" is found in the poetical book of love, The Song of Solomon: "My beloved put his hand by the hole of the door, and my bowels were moved for him." Once again the literal translation of the word is not clear. Its meaning is ". . . and my passions stirred because of him." Song of Sol. 5:4, KJV.

SATAN

Now we turn the light of the Aramaic language upon one of the most misunderstood subjects in the Bible, the malevolent force known as Satan. The idiomatic terms, "Satan," "Devil," "evil spirit," and "unclean spirit" are extensively used in the New Testament. Although there are a few such references in the Old Testament, it is Jesus and the apostles who make use of these idioms most frequently. There are also many similar expressions used in our own language which do not actually refer to an invisible creature called Satan or the Devil, such as "the devil with you!" "deviled ham," or jokingly, "You devil, you!" It is not my purpose in this chapter to teach the origin of Lucifer, but rather to look at the idiomatic use of such terms, which we may have taken literally when reading the teaching of Jesus or the apostles. (See Chapter 6, SYMBOLISM—The Origin of Lucifer.)

"And lest I should be exalted . . . there was given to me a thorn in the flesh, the messenger of Satan to buffet me . . ." 2 Cor. 12:7, KJV. Wherever the apostle Paul traveled, he met constant opposition and verbal attacks against his "apostolic authority." Evidently, after he preached in certain areas, false teachers arrived, accusing him of disreputable leadership and throwing doubt on his "apostleship." These accusations vexed and annoyed Paul and were a continual source of irritation to him, "a thorn in flesh."[6] Many passages of Scripture make use of the idiom, "thorn," —for example, Gen. 3:18, Num. 33:55, Judges 2:3, and Josh. 23:13.

In modern English, Paul would have said, "I'm plagued with troublemakers," for the expression, "messenger of Satan," denotes a troublemaker, that is, a false, deceptive teacher who causes people to miss the mark or to go astray with misleading philosophies or teachings. In this case, the malicious talk was ruining his reputation.

In a letter to Timothy, Paul says, "of whom is Hymenaeos and Alexander; whom I have delivered unto Satan, that they may learn not to blaspheme." 1 Tim. 1:20, KJV. In the Near East, the expression "to deliver people to Satan" means "to turn them over to their own devices," or "to let them stew in their own juices." In English we would say, "Give them enough rope and they will hang themselves."[7]

In First Corinthians, the fifth chapter, there is a report of an immorality charge against a son who slept with one of his father's wives. (Bear in mind that polygamy is practiced in the Near East.) Paul tells the Corinthians to gather in Jesus' name and deliver that person to Satan, ". . . to deliver such a one unto Satan for the destruction of the flesh that the spirit may be saved in the day of the Lord Jesus." 1 Cor. 5:5, KJV. How can one be handed over to Satan and yet retain a promise of being "saved in the day of the Lord Jesus?" Turning to Aramaic-Semitic idioms to unravel the mystery, we learn that Paul meant to let the man "stew" in his own evil acts, or to deliver him to his own misdeeds. A similar English idiom would be "Let him rot in hell." But why did Paul give such a strong imperative? Had he no pity? On the contrary, this is why the last part of the verse reads, "that the spirit may be saved in the day of the Lord Jesus." Evidently, some people only learn their lessons through the suffering brought on by their own harmful actions. Thus, after reaching a certain level in their self-destructive habits, they wake up, cease what they are doing, turn from their harmful acts, and are "saved" from further evil and suffering.[8]

The Term "Devil"

The term "devil" refers to being "crazy" or "insane." An insane person or a crazy action was called "devil." Idol worship, for instance, was considered devil worship by the Hebrews. They believed it was "crazy" or "insane" to worship an idol, reasoning that since idols were made by man, there could be no life in them. Yet idols of stone and wood were venerated, bowed to, and kissed by their worshippers. To the Hebrews, this was "crazy," hence, "devil-worship." On the occasion, certain religious authorities became angry and said to Jesus, "Say we not well, that thou art a Samaritan and that thou hast a devil?" John 8:48, KJV. They meant, "You are not a true adherent to the Jewish faith and you are crazy."

The mentally and emotionally ill of that day were considered to be "devils" or "devil-possessed." Their speech and actions were not normal, so people said they had "evil or unclean spirits." In the biblical days people with uncontrollable tempers were thought to be demon-possessed. Many times Jesus spoke to and cured these "devils" (the mentally ill). One man told Jesus that his name was "Legion," meaning he had "many devils," that is, many things wrong with him.

It was said of Mary of Magdala that she had "seven devils," which meant she was really "into" her erroneous ways. Seven is a sacred number, and it is believed that if one has seven of anything, it is complete.

Actually, Mary would not have needed seven devils to do the job. One would have been sufficient. Then again, seven devils implies seven crazy thoughts or seven detrimental habits. Mary needed help and Jesus healed her. She was filled with gratitude and became a devoted follower of Jesus and his teaching.

There is no doubt that Jesus' spiritual essence manifested in a powerfully magnetic and dynamic way. His presence and peacefulness exerted a strong influence over the physically and mentally ill, for he had absolute confidence in the healing and restorative powers of God in man.

In his gospel, Luke tells us about the return of the seventy disciples and of their successful healing ministry and mission. They were excited and exuberant because the physically ill had been healed, and in their words, ". . . our Lord, even the devils are subject unto us through thy name." Luke 10:17, KJV. That is, the mentally and emotionally ill responded to Jesus' method of healing through his disciples. Jesus rejoiced over their success and said to them, "I beheld Satan as lightning fall from heaven." Luke 10:18, KJV. This is idiomatic speech and means "I saw truth conquering evil." "To fall from heaven," in Semitic terms, signifies "losing one's power and influence."

There is a prophecy in which Isaiah declares to the king of Babylon "How are you fallen from heaven," denoting that the monarch would lose his kingdom. Isaiah 14:12–22. By the same token, "to rise to heaven" means "to gain in power and influence." Jesus knew his powerful truth would triumph over all so-called "evil" forces and influences. The simple disciples were filled with the Word of truth, love, and power that transformed the hearts and minds of people. They demonstrated the kingdom of God on earth.

CONCLUSION

Recognizing and understanding idioms in any language is very important, especially if one desires to communicate well and to comprehend what others mean. The same principle applies to the Scriptures. Now we can see how vital the second key is in unlocking many passages of the Bible.

CHAPTER 3

The Third Key
Mysticism

The Bible reports two forms of mysticism: the mundane and the spiritual. Mundane mysticism is knowledge gained through personal, subjective experience of insight and intuition. Spiritual mysticism is a way of "knowing" that transcends ordinary circumstances and the physical appearance of persons, places, and things. In other words, it is "knowledge" discerned through transpersonal, transcendental realizations. It is a level of consciousness whereby we are able to perceive the phenomenal world from a metaphysical perspective. In philosophical terms, this level of awareness; i.e., perception, is known as a noumenon.

MYSTICISM: A MUNDANE EXAMPLE

A good biblical example of mundane mysticism is found in 1 Samuel 9:1-20. A young Israelite of the Benjamite tribe, named Saul, was searching for his father's donkeys but he and his servant could not find them. So they decided to seek help from the prophet Samuel. Before Saul and his servant could even question the seer, Samuel told them that the donkeys were found and now Saul's father was

34

worried about them. Samuel was clairvoyant and therefore, through his psychic power and inner sight, was able to "know" the whereabouts of the animals. A mundane problem for Saul and his servant was solved by the psychic sensitivity of the Hebrew seer and judge of Israel.

MYSTICISM: A SPIRITUAL EXAMPLE

The opening chapter of Genesis is a good example of spiritual mysticism. It is a spiritual revelation of creation and not a "Western scientific treatise." If we, as contemporary readers of the creation account, wish to understand this kind of writing, we must be drawn into the intent and atmosphere of the writer. However, this cannot be done if we attempt to impose our modern "scientific minds" upon the text. The biblical writer is not interested in, nor is he trying to prove scientifically, the existence of God and the spiritual origin of man and the universe. To him these ideas were the facts! His conviction came by revelation; that is, through a transpersonal, transcendental realization within his own heart and mind.

The esoteric, spiritual revelation of creation is meaningful only to those whose hearts and minds are open to and perceptive of spiritual realities and unseen forces of our magnificent cosmos. The account of creation is a masterpiece of subtle metaphor and vivid imagery, which cannot be fully appreciated by biblical literalists, modern materialists, or pseudo-intellectuals. It is best understood and interpreted from an intuitive level. (A detailed account of the creation story is given in my book *The Mysteries of Creation*.)

DREAMS AND VISIONS

Dreams, visions and revelations play a major role in the Bible. For instance, when God revealed himself to the prophets and patriarchs, He usually did so through dreams, visions and revelations. How do we know this? The Scriptures testify to this fact in various places. This does not imply, however, that dreams and visions were the only means for spiritual guidance and communication.

In the book of Job, for example, we are told, "For God speaks once; he does not speak a second time; *through a dream* and *through a vision* of the night, when sleep falls upon men, while in deep slumber upon the bed, then he opens the ears of men . . ." Job 33:14–16, Aramaic text.

Moses also explains to us the method by which God made Himself known to the prophets: "And the Lord said to them, Hear now my words: If you are prophets I the Lord *will reveal myself to you in a vision* and *will speak to you in a dream.*" Numbers 12:6, Aramaic text. The psalmist declares: "For the Lord is our hope; and the Holy One of Israel is our King. Then He spoke *in visions* to His righteous one, and He said . . ." Psalms 89:18–19, Aramaic text.

When King Solomon prayed for wisdom, the scribe who chronicled the king's reign reports, "In Gibeon the Lord appeared to Solomon *in a dream* by night and God said, Ask that I shall give thee." 1 Kings 3:5, KJV. There are many other verses that substantiate dreams and visions as God's means of communication.

Over forty percent of the Hebrew Scripture is based on dreams, visions and revelations. The astounding appearances of God and angels usually occurred in the minds of the Hebrew people while they were sleeping or in a deep trance. Spiritual ideas and illumination were received by all the prophets through dreams. As far as we know, none of the patriarchs carried any holy books with them for guidance or instruction, for the Word of God manifested itself in their hearts and minds via dreams and visions. Thus the Bible came as a result of the patriarchs' "living" encounters with spiritual forces. The Spirit of truth wrote on the "tables of their hearts" and not on the "skins of sheep."

Jesus himself relied on the dreams and visions of the prophets to guide him through his role as the Messiah (Christ). Jesus quotes Isaiah more than any other prophet. He studied the revelations of Isaiah and patterned his life according to the dreams and predictions of this great prophet and statesman.

THE MEANING OF THE WORD *Dream*

Our English word "dream" comes from Medieval English and early Teutonic roots and means "to deceive." But in all three Semitic tongues, Aramaic, Hebrew, and Arabic, the root of the word has an amazingly different meaning.

KHELMA, "dream," comes from *KHLM* and means "to heal," "to make well or whole," and "to integrate." In other words, when the ancient Semitic people used the word "dream," they were attempting to explain the strange phenomenon that occurs during sleep. Evidently they understood the process to be some sort of healing, guiding, and integrating mechanism of the mind, as many psychologists and psychiatrists of today have recognized.

KEY EXPRESSIONS

When we read the Bible, how can we tell whether we are reading a mystical incident or an historical event? There are key phrases which can help us recognize the difference between the psychical and historical events. In many passages, the writers plainly state that the occurrence is a dream or a vision. Sometimes an author may not explicitly say so, but will use one of the following expressions:

The angel of the Lord appeared. . . .
I was in the Spirit (trance). . . .
The Spirit of the Lord was upon me. . . .
The word of the Lord came to me saying, and I saw. . . .
The Lord God appeared to Moses in. . . .

There are also times when no specific key phrase introduces a mystical event. When this occurs, the only way to discern the happening is to realize that whenever God and men, or angels and men, or God and angels are holding a conversation, the incident may safely be understood as a dream or a vision.

Interestingly, the word "to appear," *ETHGLI*, in Aramaic, means "to come by revelation." *ETH* means "to come" and *GLI* means "to reveal," "to unveil," and "to uncover." Hence, it means "to come in a vision or a dream," especially with a preceding phrase such as *"And the angel of the Lord appeared."* One may also translate this bibilical phrase thus: *"And the angel of the Lord came by revelation to . . ."*

We are now ready to study some passages of the Bible that possibly have been understood as literal events rather than as visions or dreams.

ABRAHAM

Moses describes an experience of Abraham, the Hebrew patriarch, which tested him severely. "And it came to pass after these things that *God did tempt Abraham* . . . And He said take now your son, your only son Isaac, whom you love . . . And offer him there for a burnt offering . . ." Gen. 22:1-2, KJV. This is very difficult to understand and it also raises a few questions in our minds. Does God tempt His faithful devotees? Was God interested in human sacrifice? Was the God of Abraham just like the pagan gods who demanded sacrifice for appeasement?

James, the brother of Jesus, writes in his epistle the following statement, "Let no man say when he is tempted, I am tempted of God; for God cannot be tempted with evil, neither does He tempt any man." James 1:13, KJV. How is it that the apostle James says God does not tempt man and yet Moses says that "God did tempt Abraham?" We can understand. this seeming contradiction by realizing that Abraham was dreaming. He felt that God wanted his son as a sacrifice, but as the dream progressed it was revealed to Abraham that God does not need nor demand human sacrifice. In other words, Abraham was guided by God in a dream never to practice pagan rites of human sacrifice. He also learned from his dream that he did love God above all else. So this was a lesson to be passed on to the future generations of Israel. Again, we must keep in mind that at that time there were no holy books or written laws among the Hebrews. The people were guided by Father Abraham and by his spiritually informative dreams. Basically, the biblical author narrates Abraham's visions and dreams more than the chronological, physical events of the patriarch's life. It is interesting to note that even after Israel had the books of Moses, the great seers and prophets of the Bible were taught by God through dreams and visions.

MAR NARSAI

One of the early Aramaic-speaking Church Fathers, known as Mar Narsai, also tells us in his commentaries that God appeared to the patriarchs and prophets in dreams and visions. Mar Narsai belonged to the Aramaic-speaking branch of the early Christian Church. He was a theologian, prolific writer and commentator on the Bible. The probable date of his birth was 399 A.D. He became the head of the famous biblical Aramaic school of Edessa.

Mar Narsai in his writings explained many difficult passages of the Bible. His knowledge of the Aramaic language, customs, manners, metaphors, and allegories enabled him to unlock many portions of the Scriptures which have been difficult for us in the Western world to understand. He was very aware of the fact that many of the biblical episodes were based on God's visions to the Hebrew patriarchs and prophets. The following is a translation from the writings of Mar Narsai. It is a literal rendering of Aramaic texts of the writings of Mar Narsai with some additional English words put in parentheses to help clarify the meaning of the sentence.

GOD'S APPEARANCE TO ABRAHAM

In a still vision He (God) revealed His will to His beloved friend. And he conversed with Him pleasantly according to his understanding . . .

It was not by the means of something expected but *in a vision* and as the appearance of a man that Abraham saw God and he (Abraham) received Him in his house as a man who can be seen. As a man, he received Him and not humanly because it is impossible to see God with the human eye. It was not God's (spiritual) nature that Abraham saw *in his vision* but in a mystery he conversed with His body alone. Yet Abraham could not see it in reality. It was not reality which took place in the house of Abraham, but rather mystery which cannot be explained by those who are endowed only by the power of speech. The nature of God cannot be described by those who are endowed by the power of speech alone. Thus what is written cannot be described literally. It was not (in a) corporeal (sense) that Abraham refreshed (God) with eating and drinking . . . It was figurative all that took place in that revelation with Abraham, a human vision, human speech and human food. God performed all of this very wisely as is the custom of his power to perform in all generations.[1]

God Dines with Abraham

The encounter between God and Abraham in the 18th chapter of Genesis is written in a very warm and human style. God reveals himself to Abraham as an Eastern tribal chieftain. According to the biblical record, Abraham was at his tent door. He had fallen asleep, and as he awoke in his dream he saw three men coming down the road. It was God and two angels. They were on their way to Sodom and Gomorrah, but it was growing late so Abraham in a typical Eastern manner approached the three men. He begged them seven times to rest themselves under the tree so that he might wash their feet and bring them some water and a morsel of bread to sustain their hearts. Abraham served them cakes from the griddle, veal, and some buttermilk which was a form of yogurt.

The Lord God revealed to Abraham that he and his wife Sarah were to have a child in about a year. Sarah, who was hiding by the tent door and listening to the conversation, laughed when she heard God make the statement that she was to have a child. The Lord God had heard Sarah laughing and called her to come forward. He questioned her about her laughter. She quickly denied the fact that she had laughed at his prophecy. Sarah was embarrassed. Nonetheless, the Lord God assured her she was going to have a child anyway!

The beauty and warmth of this particular story depicts the type of relationship which existed between Abraham and his God. Can you imagine yourself daydreaming about the Lord God of heaven and earth and sitting down and dining with you, and then continuing to dream that your wife laughed and couldn't believe what the Lord God had declared! It is no wonder that Abraham was called a ''friend of

God!'' This was not a relationship of fear. It was one of friendship and love. The inner workings and soul of Abraham are clearly revealed to us by his dreams. By studying the dreams of Abraham we see the consciousness of Abraham unfolding in many ways. His dreams are very commonplace, very plain, simple and direct. Thus, the mysticism we find in the life of Abraham is not one of mystery or dark sayings. His revelations were simple and clear.

MOSES

The mysticism of Moses, the great lawgiver and prophet, is very different from that of Abraham. Moses was brought up in the magnificent land and fabulous courts of Egypt, so his visions and his dreams have the touch of the Egyptian splendor and majesty. God appears to Moses in a burning bush, and he was told to remove the shoes from his feet, for the ground on which he stood was holy. In the revelations of Moses we come to realize that he is acting as God's counselor; God is the great king needing advice from his wise advisor. This is why we find so many recorded events of conversations between God and Moses very intriguing. But why would God take advice from Moses? The answer is simple. These are Moses' dreams.

There is an amazing and incredible passage in the book of Exodus, Chapter 33, verses 1-4, which serves as an outstanding example of God's acting out the role of a king. The Lord God calls Moses up into the mountain and speaks to him saying:

> . . . Depart, and go up hence, thou and the people which thou hast brought up out of the land of Egypt, unto the land which I sware unto Abraham, to Isaac, and to Jacob, saying, Unto thy seed will I give it; And I will send an angel before thee; and I will drive out the Canaanite, the Amorite, and the Hittite, and

the Perizzite, the Hivite, and the Jebusite; Unto a land flowing with milk and honey; for I will not go up in the midst of thee; for thou are a stiffnecked people, lest I consume thee in the way. And when the people heard these evil tidings, they mourned; and no man did put on him his ornaments. Ex. 33:1–4, KJV.

Moses' communication with the Lord God took place in a vision, and the conversation must not be taken literally. God was not angry or discouraged, but it is written this way for a reason. Let's look at the text. It seems to say that God is worn out and disgusted with Israel's unruly, rebellious, and disobedient behavior. He is so incensed by the twelve tribes that he has decided not to go with them into Palestine. God is also so discouraged that he places the blame on Moses for bringing the people out of Egypt, wanting Moses to bear the responsibility of leading these obstinate, "stiffnecked" people (according to the Scripture) into the promised land. In other words, God seems to be admitting that even He cannot guide and govern such a stubborn people.

Later on in the episode Moses implores God to go with Israel. Even though God has assured Moses of sending an angel to take his place, Moses is still unwilling to continue without God Himself. Finally, God consents to go.

Is this possible? Was the Creator of the universe angry, helpless and unable to rule His people? Looking only on the surface of the incident, God appears as a weak and discouraged leader, though we know that God is not weak, nor is there anything which is impossible for the Creator. Why is it written this way?

Biblical writers were skilled at delivering spiritual ideas in human terms. They often characterized God as a shepherd feeding his flock or as an eagle protecting little ones under its wings. Sometimes they described God as being angry, happy, sorry or disappointed.

In this particular incident God is depicted as being very

angry so that Moses can reveal how extremely difficult it has been for him to guide and discipline these tribal people during the exodus and travel through the desert. We must keep in mind that in those days it took a tremendous amount of courage and powerful leadership to unite twelve rivaling Semitic tribes. According to biblical history, inter-tribal rivalry continued among the Israelites until the Assyrians carried away ten of the twelve tribes into the North. What an unforgettable legacy this biblical passage was for the descendants of Israel—describing Israel's forefathers as being so obstinate that even God could not take it! This was a valuable lesson for future generations so that they would not repeat the same patterns and disobey God's laws.

JOSHUA

The Lord God said to Joshua, the son of Nun, Moses' minister, "Moses my servant is dead; now therefore arise, go over this Jordan, thou, and all this people, into the land which I do give to them, even to the children of Israel." Joshua 1:2, KJV. Joshua dreamed about God. The Lord appeared to him in visions leading him and guiding him as the captain of the hosts with a drawn sword, just like any other military leader.

> And it came to pass, when Joshua was by Jericho, that he lifted up his eyes and looked, and, behold, there stood a man over against him with his sword drawn in his hand, and Joshua went unto him, and said unto him, Art thou for us, of for our adversaries? And he said, Nay; but as captain of the host of the Lord am I now come. And Joshua fell on his face to the earth, and did worship, and said unto him, What saith my lord unto his servant? Joshua 5:13–14, KJV.

Almost all leaders in Israel were guided by dreams and visions. There were Deborah, the prophetess; Samson's mother; Gideon; the young boy, Samuel; Nathan and many other prophets who guided the kings in Israel. Let us consider two major Hebrew prophets, Jonah and Ezekiel.

JONAH

Some prophets warned of wars and other major political events. But other prophets, like Jonah, experienced states of expanded consciousness.

> Now the word of the Lord came unto Jonah the son of Amittai, saying, Arise, go to Nineveh, that great city, and cry against it; for their wickedness is come up before me. Jonah 1:1-2, KJV.

The prophet Jonah made his appearance some time during the 8th century B.C., but no biblical authority knows the date for certain. Be that as it may, Jonah had received a revelation, a divine commission to go to Nineveh, the capitol of Assyria, and to predict its downfall. Jonah, instead of obeying the voice, boarded a ship at Joppa and had hoped to flee to Spain, but a mighty storm occurred at sea, and the ship and all aboard were in grave danger.

The crew, being fearful, drew lots to see why this terrible fate had befallen them. The lot fell upon Jonah. After the crew interrogated the prophet, the sailors became even more fearful. Every man on the ship tried to bring the vessel back to land, but to no avail. Finally, Jonah instructed the crew to throw him overboard. The crew prayed and asked that this deed they were about to do would not be held against them; then they threw the prophet into the sea. Immediately he was swallowed by a fish. While imprisoned in the belly of the fish, the prophet prayed and repented. Then the Lord God had the fish cast Jonah onto the dry land.

The prophet went to Nineveh, prophesied to the Assyrians and told them of the impending disaster. The Ninevites repented of their wrongs, and God spared the city. Because of God's loving kindness, Jonah's prediction did not come to pass. This disturbed the prophet because it made him appear as a false seer. The fact is that Jonah had suspected all along that God's mercy, compassion and graciousness might be bestowed upon the Assyrians, and that is exactly what God did for the Ninevites (See Jonah 4:1-3).

A question that is usually asked concerning this prophecy is, "Was Jonah really swallowed by a fish?" The Scripture says, "Now the Lord had prepared a great fish to swallow up Jonah. And Jonah was in the belly of the fish three days and three nights." Jonah 1:17, KJV.

First, it is necessary to establish the theme of Jonah's message regardless of whether one considers the account as a dream or as an actual event in the prophet's life. It must be clearly understood that the object of the story was to reveal the universal presence of God. It is also made known that God's mercy and care are for all nations and not for the Hebrews alone. In other words, God wants justice, love and peace for all people.

Second, the phrase, "The word of the Lord came to Jonah," indicates that this episode was a vision. Jonah was to learn a valuable lesson. He would transcend both nationalism and contemporary Hebrew beliefs and come to understand the spiritual value of life and God's care for all mankind. Jonah's vision would be the means through which this universal truth would be taught, not only to the Hebrews, but to all those who would read and grasp the spiritual import of this powerful revelation.

Now, as for exactly what took place regarding Jonah, Near Eastern interpreters regard this incident as having happened in a dream. Dreams, or visions of the night, can often seem to be a physical reality and, no doubt, Jonah must have experienced this apparent reality. Had this event not transpired in a psychic state, the author would have said, "And there came a large fish and swallowed him," but instead the author uses the key phrase, "Now the Lord had prepared a great fish to swallow up Jonah . . . ," which implies an altered state of consciousness; i.e., dream state. Many sincere Bible students have wondered how Jonah could have known that three days and three nights had passed while he was inside the fish. He couldn't see the sun rise or set! This is a good indication that the event was not literally true.

Another key point to consider is the fact that according to Eastern dream interpretation a fish symbolizes trouble or sorrow. The Semitic idiom, "to be in a fish," means "to be in a quandary or a dilemma." Even to this day, Eastern people often say, "He is in the bottom of the sea;" and in some dialects of Aramaic it is said, "He is in the ear of a fish." Our English equivalent to describe Jonah's plight would be, "He is in a pickle," "in a jam," "in hot water" or "He is in over his head." Interestingly, the name *Nineveh* is derived from the fish god, *Ninos*. The ancient Assyrians worshipped the fish as one of their gods.[2]

Great enlightenment dawned in Jonah's heart and mind, and through his dream he came to an all-inclusive realization of the universality of God.

Modern interpreters look upon the story of Jonah as either a parable or an allegory. Parables are considered by Eastern authorities to be much more graphic, forceful, and appealing than a plain statement of doctrine. Regardless of how one may interpret this story, the essential teaching is that the Gentiles should not be begrudged God's love, care, and forgiveness.

EZEKIEL

> Now it came to pass in the thirtieth year, in the
> fourth month, in the fifth day of the month, as I was
> among the captives by the river of Chebar, that the
> *heavens were opened,* and *I saw visions of God.* In
> the fifth day of the month, which was the fifth year
> of King Jehoiachin's captivity, *The word of the Lord
> came expressly unto* Ezekiel the priest. Ezekiel
> 1:1-3, KJV.

There are three phrases here that introduce the mystical
episode in Ezekiel's prophecy: "heavens were opened," "I
saw visions of God," and "the word of the Lord came to."
In Semitic languages, "the heavens were opened" is an
expression one finds quite frequently throughout the Old
and New Testaments. It means "a revelation is being
disclosed."

While Ezekiel was being held prisoner by the river Che-
bar, some strange creatures visited him in a vision. The
prophet looked and beheld:

> . . . a whirlwind came out of the north, a great
> cloud, and a fire unfolding itself, and a brightness
> was about it, and out of the midst thereof as the col-
> our of amber, out of the midst of the fire. Also out of
> the midst thereof came the likeness of four living
> creatures. And this was their appearance; they had
> the likeness of a man. And every one had four faces,
> and every one had four wings. . . . As for the like-
> ness of their faces, they four had the face of a man,
> and the face of a lion, on the right side; and they four
> had the face of an ox on the left side; they four also
> had the face of an eagle. Ezekiel 1:4-10, KJV.

These verses have led to many unusual conclusions.
Some believe that Ezekiel was seeing a jet airliner, and

others have believed he was describing a UFO. All these ideas aside, surely Ezekiel was seeing something that had meaning for the people of his day. What were these strange creatures, and what was the meaning of this phenomenon? What were the events that led to this mysterious vision?

The Hebrew prophets, Jeremiah and Ezekiel, had predicted that Jerusalem would be conquered and destroyed by the Chaldean armies. These two courageous men of God had disagreed with the policy of the court prophets in Jerusalem because it favored an alliance with Egypt, Syria and other adjacent countries. The kings of Judah did not know which way to turn. The State was weak, caught between two powerful imperial nations.

When Nebuchadnezzar, king of Babylon, discovered that the State of Judah had broken its alliance with him by making a secret treaty with Egypt, he invaded Palestine. King Nebuchadnezzar's armies captured Jerusalem, dethroned Jehoiachin, and replaced him with one of his brothers. During this invasion the armies carried away many princes, generals, men of nobility and artists. Then suddenly the news came that Egyptian troops were marching into Palestine, and Nebuchadnezzar's forces had to retreat.

Jeremiah and Ezekiel were mocked by the false court prophets who firmly believed that the king of Babylon would not be victorious, although Ezekiel was certain Nebuchadnezzar would return and conquer all of Palestine. Now, it was at this crucial period when Ezekiel was a prisoner of the invading Chaldean army, that the "strange creatures" made their appearance to the prophet in a vision foretelling the impending final disaster which was to befall both Palestine and Egypt.

In his vision he saw the strange creatures come out of a whirlwind. They were shaped like some kind of vehicle with wings and wheels. On the rims of the wheels were human eyes, and under the wings were human hands. The creatures had four faces—those of a man, a lion, an ox and an eagle. They had many other distinctive features as well (See Ezekiel, Chapter 1).

These strange creatures symbolize the greatest war machine ever mobilized in the history of the ancient world. Nebuchadnezzar was preparing to march against Judah and Egypt for the second time. The wings of the creatures denoted the speed of the invading cavalry, riding Arabian horses which were swift as eagles. "When the living creatures were lifted up from the ground, the wheels were lifted up with them," says the prophet. This means that when the cavalry went forward, the infantry followed. "Their rims were full of eyes" indicates intelligence. That is, the army was guided by strategists, astrologers, engineers, soothsayers and other men who were trained in tactical warfare.

"Wherever the spirit was to go, they went, . . ." means that wherever the intelligence officers directed the invading forces to go they would go. "And they went everyone straight forward, . . ." tells that they would not retreat. The army would not change its direction until complete victory was attained. The face of a man indicates intellect. That of a lion symbolizes dominion. The ox denotes endurance and strength, and the eagle depicts speed and omnipresence.

Ezekiel's vision revealed that even though the king of Babylon had retreated after his first invasion he was not defeated. Rather, he was making even greater preparations to carry out his threat against the nations beyond the river Euphrates by preparing an army with supplies and water that would last for years. When the second invasion did come, Babylonian forces slew Pharaoh Neco, captured Jerusalem, carried away the rich treasury, burned the city and uprooted the holy temple just as Jeremiah and Ezekiel had predicted. Thus, the vision had meaning for the people in those days. The prophetic vision served as a warning so that Israel could be prepared and avoid being caught between two great powers, Egypt and Babylon.[3]

THE NEW TESTAMENT

Let us now move on to the New Testament. The first episode of mysticism we encounter is the annunciation, the appearance of Gabriel to Mary, the mother of Jesus. The visitation of the angel to Mary is not an unusual occurrence in the Near East even to this very day. Married women who have a difficult time in conceiving generally make a special pilgrimage to certain shrines, holy places, churches, mosques, sacred mountain tops or any place where they might feel the presence of God and know that their request will be answered. They will wait until "a presence" is revealed, i.e., a dream or a vision be granted to them. Generally an angel or a patron saint will appear in a dream and announce that the petitioners will become pregnant, and sometimes the angel will also name the child that is to be born. This occurrence still happens in many places in the Near East today.[4]

According to the New Testament, the angel Gabriel appeared to Mary, the same Gabriel that appeared to Daniel and to Mohammed. "Gabriel" in Aramaic means "man of God." "Angel" means "counselor" or "God's thought." An angel is the presence of God counseling an individual who may be receiving the dream or vision.

THE VISITATION

"Now in the sixth month the angel Gabriel was sent from God to Galilee, to the city named Nazareth." Luke 1:26, Aramaic text. Thus Luke opens his account of the angelic visitation to Mary which was to announce the conception of Jesus. There are a few matters for us to understand before we proceed any further. First of all, we must realize that we are faced with Eastern mysticism. We must also recognize that Mary was in an altered state of consciousness when this appearance took place.

The prophetic word from spiritual realms was manifesting itself in Mary's heart and mind in what we know today as a "thought form." Luke continues his narrative telling us, "And upon entering the angel said to her, Peace to you, O full of grace; our Lord is with you, O blessed among women. . . . And the angel said to her, 'Don't be afraid, Mary; for you have found grace with God.' " Luke 1:28–30, Aramaic text. To our minds this entire episode seems strange, but not to the Eastern mind, for there is absolutely nothing strange about it, nor is there a single aspect of it that is not in "perfect harmony with the prevailing modes of thought, customs and speech of the Near East."[5]

To this very day Easterners talk about "heavenly messengers" in the form of patron saints or of angels coming to the pious, childless wives in dreams and visions and encouraging them with the promise of motherhood. As I stated earlier, many Eastern wives fast and pray until "the presence" is revealed, that is, until an angel manifests in a dream and brings the good news of conception.

In the East conception is considered "sacred" and "blessed." Semitic people believe that human reproduction is profoundly holy, for it is "God's life reproducing itself in the life of man."[6] There is also no way to describe the reproach an Eastern wife feels if she cannot conceive and remains "barren." Thus, for an angel to greet a woman with the words, "Grace" or "full of grace" in a dream would signify that divine favor is upon "the blessed woman," since to an Easterner children are a heritage from the Lord, and every conception and birth is miraculous.[7]

And, behold, thou shalt conceive in thy womb, and bring forth a son, and shalt call his name Jesus. He shall be great, and shall be called the Son of the Highest; and the Lord God shall give unto him the throne of his father David; And he shall reign over the house of Jacob for ever; and of his kingdom there shall be no end. Luke 1:31–33, KJV.

The angel Gabriel reveals to Mary that the son she is about to conceive must be named Jesus, i.e., "Savior." Furthermore, the angelic visitor predicts that the child, *"shall be called* the Son of the Highest." The question often asked is, "Why didn't the angel say, He *is* the Son of the Highest?"

> . . . Both the angel and the author of the gospel knew the customs and temperament of Eastern people, especially the Jews. To call a man the Son of God implies that the God of the Jews was married as the pagan gods were. This is blasphemy and is considered a pagan doctrine. God is spirit, life and truth; and these attributes are not subject to conception and birth. Jesus called God his Father, and he is known as God's son in a spiritual and not in a physical sense. . . . [8]

Thus the angel declares prophetically that Jesus is to demonstrate divine sonship and therefore *will be called* the "Son of the Highest." His sonship was marked by the truth he revealed, the healings he manifested and by his own miraculous resurrection from the tomb and recovery from death.

Gabriel further predicts that the messianic kingdom will have no boundaries. In those ancient days the people of Palestine considered the Euphrates River and the Mediterranean Sea the ends of the world. Since Eastern kings were known by the size of their realms, their ambition was to extend the boundaries of their kingdoms, for the larger the territory the more famous the king.

The kingdom of the Christ, however, is a spiritual domain, and therefore limitless. It embraces the entire world, including people of all races and countries. Not only does this kingdom transcend earthly, man-made boundaries and kingdoms, it also transcends space and time. No ruler of this world, past or present, has ever been able to create such a kingdom; but to the rule and supremacy of the Christ there will be no limit, for this kingdom dissolves all barriers of time, race and geography.

Easterners believe God participates in the act of procreation in the sense that he allows the woman to become pregnant. "And God blessed them, and God said to them, Be fruitful and multiply, and fill the earth, and subdue it; and have dominion over the fish of the sea and over the birds of the sky, and over the cattle, and over all wild beasts that move upon the earth." Gen. 1:28, Aramaic text.

Interestingly, there is no mention of any dreams that Jesus may have had, but we do know that he was clairvoyant and made predictions (See Matt. 24). However, the basic ministry of Jesus was to fulfill the messianic office. Thus his life was the fulfillment of the visions and dreams of the Hebrew prophets.

THE BOOK OF ACTS

In the Acts of the apostles there are numerous episodes dealing with mysticism. The expansion of the early church and its missionary endeavors were not guided by boards or committees but by intuition, dreams and spiritual revelations. For example, the apostle Paul while on his way to Bithynia had a dream. A Macedonian man appeared to him and said, "Come to us in Macedonia." When he awoke the next morning, instead of going on to Bithynia, he left for

Macedonia. He was obedient to his dream (See Acts 16:1-10).

PETER'S VISION

The apostle Simon (Peter) about noontime went up on the housetop to pray. The Scriptures say that he became very hungry and wanted to eat. But while the women were preparing food for him, he fell into a trance. It is generally the custom in the East that while women are baking bread or preparing meals, the men impatiently wait on the housetop to escape the smoke from the ovens and to pass the time away. In the Near East the housetops serve as the playground and meeting place for children and men. Occasionally, because of the long wait and the aroma of the bread or other fresh foods coming up with the smoke to the rooftop, it increases the hunger of the men who are waiting.

Evidently, Peter was very hungry and he fell into a trance state. He saw a large sheet coming down from the sky full of all kinds of animals. Since Peter had fallen asleep when he was hungry, the first thing he heard the voice say to him in his vision was, "slay and eat." But Peter refused, for in typical Eastern fashion he replied, "Far be it, my Lord; for I have never eaten anything which was unclean and defiled." The term "unclean" means foods which were forbidden by the Mosaic law. But the voice came to him a second time and insisted that he should rise up, kill and eat because what God has cleansed should not be called unclean. And it happened three times.

When Peter awoke from his vision, he was bewildered and wondered what his dream meant. While the apostle was contemplating the vision, he heard a voice say to him, "Behold, three men seek you. Arise, go down and go with them, without doubt in your mind; for I have sent them."

Peter had a clairaudient experience; that is, he was guided by a voice without knowing or seeing a physical body. He was obedient to the voice, went downstairs and saw the men. These men were sent from the house of Cornelius, and Peter soon learned that the Gentiles were ready to embrace the gospel of his Lord.

I have cited only two examples of mysticism from the book of Acts but there are many more psychic episodes than just these two references. The expansion program of the early Christian Church was activated by a spiritual movement of inner impressions, inner voices, dreams, visions, and revelations.

THE BOOK OF THE REVELATION

And in conclusion, I must at least mention the last book of the New Testament known as Revelation. This book is a series of dreams and visions. The Aramaic word for "revelation," *GILIANA*, also means "vision" and implies "dream." Its root is *GLA*, which means "to uncover," "to lay open," "to declare," "to show," and "to make known." The visions in this magnificent and alluring book should not be taken literally. The Eastern imagery used by the author is a symbolic representation of spiritual and historical events. This imagery points to a much larger reality. As an example, Jesus is seen by the revelator as riding a white horse in the sky. (See Rev. 19:11-16). The rider is called "The Word of God." Truth always rides a "white horse;" that is, truth will always conquer. There will be no literal white horse in the sky. All these things are Eastern symbols and figures of speech.

Let us continue our journey through the Scriptures with our Seven Keys. We are now ready to unlock more passages of the Bible with the fourth key, the culture of the Near East.

CHAPTER 4

The Fourth Key
Near Eastern Culture

The study of the Near Eastern customs and manners is not only interesting but very important. A lack of understanding of the biblical culture can create mistaken impressions. Even in today's world we misunderstand many aspects of the Near Eastern culture. As an example, our major newspapers throughout the States carried descriptive articles on the funeral of Gamal Abdel Nasser (1918–1970), president of Egypt. The reporters stated that the funeral had been ''disrupted'' by the ''frenzy'' of the crowds. But in Eastern cultures the only suitable conduct to indicate your respect for the dead is to show you are overcome emotionally. If one stood in ''respectful silence'' at a funeral, this would mean he had no feeling for the dead at all, and it would be insulting. If we today still have difficulty in comprehending and understanding other cultures and have created some mistaken impressions, how much more have we misunderstood the biblical culture?

In this chapter we are going to look at some of the customs and manners of biblical times. Our approach to the Eastern culture is somewhat different from other biblical systems of study in that we are applying knowledge gained from the descendants of the ancient Assyrian people. (Please see "Introduction, the Fourth Key.")

It was only natural that this old Semitic stock (Assyrians), living where nothing had ever occurred to disturb their habits of life, should keep up the *old Semitic customs. They still lived*, or did live until the change of the great war brought about an alteration, *the life of the Old Testament*. "Bible customs," or those we call such, were, of course, not peculiar to the Hebrew, but were the common heritage of all the stock to which he belonged, and a part of the atmosphere of the land. Thus it was that a man of long experience, when asked by a youngster what books he had best study as a preparation to going out to Iraq, replied, "take the Bible first and foremost. For the politics of the country, study the Book of Judges. For the philosophy and religious thought, the Book of Job. For the social life and habits—well, add to the Bible 'The Arabian Nights,' Burton's edition, unexpurgated one!" Even in matters of costume, the customs of old time held good.[1]

Now let us consider some of the biblical customs of the Near East.

BREAD

Jesus understood very well the attitude of his people in regard to bread. That's why he said, "I am the bread of life." His listeners could immediately identify with his statement because they understood the sacredness of bread.

An Eastener will often say, "There is bread and salt between us," meaning "We are one by a solemn agreement." The phrase "bread and salt" is a sacred one, and if one wishes to be known as a base person and one unworthy of trust, let him break the covenant of bread and salt. This individual will then be stigmatized as one who "knows not the meaning of bread and salt." Certain desert bedouins will treat even their greatest enemies with profound courtesy, serving them food and protecting them with the sword and shelter—for three days only—if they made a bread and salt covenant with their enemies. (However, after three days, if the "enemy" is smart, he will flee for his life.)

Normally an Easterner will not tell a lie while bread is present on the table. Bread is thought to have a mystical sacredness because it is God's provision for one of man's basic needs. Where else could daily bread come from, but the caring, providing, loving hand of God for all men everywhere?

When Jesus speaks of himself as the bread of life, he refers to the sacredness, that is, to the goodness of his teaching, which nourishes the hearts and souls of mankind, bringing peace, prosperity, and a living, loving relationship with God who is Life Itself.

Daily Bread

An Easterner's entire life centers around God; that is, everything he does is done in the name of God. When he plants his seed into the freshly plowed ground or when he is ready to harvest his crop, even when he spreads the sheaves on the threshing floor and grinds his grain at the mill, all of it is done in the name of God. The women also knead the dough and bake the bread and serve it to their families with the sense of God's blessing. Hence the expression in the Lord's Prayer, "Give us this day our daily bread." It is a constant reminder that it is God who provides us with bread. It is a statement of deep gratitude to the Giver of all good and perfect gifts.[3]

Another way this phrase of the prayer may be translated is, "You provide us bread for our needs from day to day." The Aramaic word *LAKHMA*, "bread," also means "food." The expression "come, eat bread with me," means "Come and have a meal with me."

The daily bread is a reminder of God's presence which is ever with us and provides for all of our needs. As one poet put it:

Back of the loaf is the snowy flour;
back of the flour, the mill,
back of the mill is the wheat and the sower,
and the sun and the Father's will.[4]

Eastern bread is not formed like a long loaf of Italian or French bread. The shape is round like a very large pizza (about ten to twelve inches in diameter) and very thin like a corn tortilla. It is possible to feed forty people on one loaf of Eastern "bedouin" bread.

THE APPLE

Some biblical teachers consider the apple to be a symbol of evil; hence the apple has become known as the fruit of the fall of man. But, according to the Eastern custom nothing could be further from the truth. In the Near East, an apple is the symbol of beauty, affection and friendship. Eastern poets in their writings represent the apple as a symbol of love.

Eastern women often place their babies under the shadowy protection of the apple and fig trees for, when the sun is very hot, the shade of the apple tree is cool and refreshing. The ill and the weak often seek out the shadow of certain trees for healing, especially the apple tree. "Who is this that cometh up from the wilderness, leaning upon her beloved? I raised thee up (awakened you) under the apple tree: There thy mother brought thee forth: There she brought thee forth that bare thee." Song of Sol. 8:5, KJV.

At wedding feasts, apples and dates are the confections. An artificial tree is constructed, all of its branches being decorated with beautiful apples and dainty foods which are divided among the guests.

In the East, a man gives a woman an apple as a symbol of his love for her. Also, when a bride approaches her future home, the bridegroom stands on the roof and throws an apple to her. Usually the apple is caught by one of the young people who follow the wedding party.

Thus, in Bible lands, the apple is desired and coveted more than any other fruit. In the poetical book of love, the Song of Solomon, we read, "Refresh me with affections, *surround me with apples* because I am sick for love." Song of Sol. 2:5, Aramaic text.

Now we come to a question which is often asked by readers of the Bible: Did Adam and Eve eat an apple? It is helpful to realize that the tree of the knowledge of good and evil which appears in the garden of Eden is not to be understood as an actual fruit tree, and certainly not as an apple tree. The writer of the second and third chapters of Genesis names the tree and describes it metaphorically as "the Knowledge of good and evil." The apple was not "the culprit," nor was any particular fruit.

"The tree of knowledge" has many varying interpretations. There is a metaphysical interpretation which is interesting: When Adam and Eve partook of the knowledge of good and evil they began to "know" (perceive) life as an antagonistic dualism. The parable of Adam and Eve is a symbolic representation of humankind's mistaken perception of life. The story means that man no longer comprehends the oneness of life in its complementary and unfragmented form; life is described in terms of Spirit versus matter, birth versus death, etc. Therefore, man would live his life in conflict until his perception is radically and fundamentally transformed.

SWADDLING CLOTHES

"And she gave birth to her firstborn son, and she wrapped him in swaddling bands and laid him in a manger, because they had no room where they were lodging." Luke 2:7, Aramaic text.

A very old and common practice among the people of the Near East was the swaddling of newborn babies, and in many areas of the East this custom is still practiced today.

According to that custom, the newborn infant is bathed, gently rubbed with a very small amount of salt finely pulverized in a stone mortar for this great occasion, and then sprinkled with a powder made of dried myrtle leaves. Eastern parents believe that putting salt on the baby's body will make his flesh become firm. It also means that the parents will rear the child to be truthful.

The swaddle is a square yard of cloth to which a long narrow band is attached at one corner. The infant is wrapped in the swaddle with its arms close to its body and its legs stretched out; then the narrow band is wound around from shoulders to ankles. The infant looks like a tiny Egyptian mummy.[5] Semitic people swaddle their babies several times a day for at least six months, believing this will help their little bodies to grow straight and firm. This is also a sign that the parents will teach the child to become honest and straightforward and to be free from crookedness. As a general rule, mothers nurse their infants until two or three years of age.

In certain areas, to make a remark that a person may not have been "salted" at his birth is to arouse a great deal of trouble, for the salt symbolically represents faithfulness. Not to be salted or swaddled implies that the child was unwanted and its father unrecognized. The prophet Ezekiel makes reference to this custom in his prophecy against the citizens of Jerusalem who had been unfaithful to God and His commandments. Ezekiel reprimands, "Thus says the Lord God to Jerusalem: Your root and your nativity is of the land of Canaan; your father was an Amorite and your mother a Hittite. And as for the one who bore you, in the day that you were born she did not cut your navel, neither did she wash you with water nor did she salt your body nor wrap you in swaddling clothes at all." Ezk. 16:3–4, Aramaic text.

We can see that this custom is very important and symbolically significant. It would be only natural for the infant Jesus, at his birth, to be salted and swaddled by his parents, because Jesus was to be true to God and His word. Thus his swaddling represented loyalty and faithfulness to his heavenly Father as well as to his parents. Indeed, this custom and its spiritual meaning applied to all children who were swaddled.

UPON ENTERING A HOME

In the Near East the custom of entering a home is somewhat different than ours in the West. For instance, our hats come off when entering a home, but when entering an Eastern home, the shoes are removed and the hat remains on one's head. The "greeting" between the host and the guest is very effusive and expansive. Before knocking on the door with a staff, the guest would call out to those who are in the house with a statement such as, "Oh good dwellers of this house!" A reply from within the house would be "Most welcome. Please be good enough to come in." The guest would then immediately remove his shoes outside the threshold and perhaps rest his staff against the doorpost. The moment he enters the home he begins his profuse greetings of peace. Then he would make prolonged and solicitous questionings about the health, welfare and happiness of the family. The host, of course, would answer his questions, and if the two are fairly close, the host might say something like, "You have greatly honored me by coming into my home. I am not worthy of it. It is a blessing to have you under my roof; your presence makes our day three times as happy. This house is yours; you can burn it if you wish. My children also are at your disposal; I would sacrifice them all for your pleasure."[6] This extravagant and expansive welcome simply means "I am glad to see you. Please make yourself at home." However, an Easterner would find our Western way of welcoming rather dull. He delights in his flowery and extremely complimentary expression of affection to his guest.

Usually the guest will ask to sit in a lowly place near the door, but the host will take him by the arm and say, "No, that is impossible. You must come and sit up higher," and the host will lead him to a place close to him on a nice soft cushion. However, the guest, after a brief but very polite refusal that would usually be expressed in such terms as, "I am not worthy to sit close to you," or "I am not good enough," or "to sit near you is above my station in life," will happily "give in" to the urgings of the host.

Now you can understand what Jesus meant when he was instructing his disciples in Eastern etiquette and said, "But when thou are bidden, go and sit down in the lowest room; that when he that bade thee cometh, he may say unto thee, Friend, go up higher; then shalt thou have worship in the presence of them that sit at meat with thee. For whosoever exalteth himself shall be abased; and he that humbleth himself shall be exalted." Luke 14:10-11, KJV.

In the Book, *The Syrian Christ*, Dr. Rihbany quotes a typical invitation between a host and his guest.

Ennoble us by your presence.

I would be ennobled but I cannot accept.

That cannot be.

Yea, yea, it must be.

No, I swear against you by your friendship and by the life of God. I love just to acquaint you with my bread and salt.

I swear also that I find it impossible to accept your most gracious invitation. Your bread and salt are known to everyone.

Yea, do it just for our own good. By coming to us you come to your own home. Let us repay your bounty to us.

By the compassion of Allah, I have not bestowed any bounty upon you worth mentioning.

At this particular point in the invitation the host will seize his guest by the arm and with an emphatic, "I will not let you go," will pull at him and will drag him bodily into the house. Then the guest, happy in being vanquished with "honor," consents to the invitation.[7]

Once all the fine and elaborate Eastern etiquette is over, the guest will sit with dignified freedom next to the host, usually with his legs folded under him and his palms resting upon his knees.

TRAVELING

After these things the Lord appointed other seventy also, and sent them two and two before his face into every city and place, whither he himself would come. Therefore said he unto them, the harvest truly is great, but the labourers are few; pray ye therefore the Lord of the harvest that he would send

forth labourers into his harvest. Go your ways;
behold, I send you forth as lambs among wolves.
Carry neither purse, nor scrip, nor shoes; and salute
no man by the way. Luke 10:1–4, KJV.

To most of us in the Western world Jesus' instruction to his
disciples not to greet anyone while traveling from city to
city appears rather strange.

Easterners are very social and generally greet each other
warmly, whether they are in their home town or traveling
from place to place. Once again Dr. Abraham Rihbany details a common conversation between two strangers meeting on the road.

> The Easterner's greeting is a copious flow of soul,
> whose intimacy and inquisitiveness are very strange
> to the mentality of the West. . . .
>
> "May God (Allah) give you health and strength."
>
> "Oh, may God (Allah) refresh and strengthen your
> life."
>
> "Whence has your excellent presence come, and
> where are you facing?"
>
> "From Nazareth have I come, and I am facing Da-
> mascus."
>
> "What is the precious name?"
>
> "Your humble servant Mas'ud, son of Yusuf of the
> clan of Job, and my years, friend, are four and
> thirty."
>
> "All Honor, all honor! May your life be long and
> happy."
>
> "What children have you?"
>
> "Three sons in the keeping of God."
>
> Thus the mutually complimentary conversation and
> the searching of hearts continue until each of the

travelers is throughly informed concerning the personal, domestic, and social affairs of the other. The trade, the income, the profession, the cares and anxieties, and even the likes and dislikes of each are made known to the other before their ways part.[8]

Sometimes the traveler may also be invited to the home of the person he has just met, and it may take three or more days before the traveler may leave (See Judges 19:4–9).

But when one does not greet on the road, Easterners understand that the wayfarer is on very urgent business. Now Jesus did not want his apostles detained, as this would have delayed the spread of his gospel. Hence, his command not to salute any man on the road. The prophet Elisha gave a similar command to his servant Gehazi. The servant had a mission of healing to perform. Elisha did not want Gehazi to be detained on the road; thus he forbade him to greet anyone while he was traveling. (See 2 Kings 4:29).

Jesus had also commanded his disciples not to carry purse, scrip nor shoes. Money was usually carried in purses or in the girdle (belt) wrapped around the men. The term "scrip" means "bag," in Aramaic *TARMALA*. Eastern men usually carry their food supplies in the *TARMALA*. Carrying extra shoes or clothing would invite bandits to attack and rob them. Jesus did not want his disciples exposed to this kind of danger. They were to teach what Jesus had taught them, heal the sick, and preach that the kingdom of God had come. In return for ministering to the spiritual and physical needs of the people, the people would provide them with food, shelter, and anything else that was necessary. This was all in accord with Near Eastern custom. By remaining free of any excess baggage, the disciples could travel without fear and fulfill the commisson of their master. (See *Gospel Light*, Lamsa pp. 75–78).

WEDDING CUSTOMS

The wedding customs of the Near East are truly fascinating. In this book we will discuss only certain customs as they relate to particular teachings of the Scriptures. Let us examine the Parable of the Ten Virgins told by Jesus.

> Then shall the kingdom of heaven be likened unto ten virgins, which took their lamps, and went forth to meet the bridegroom. And five of them were wise, and five were foolish. They that were foolish took their lamps, and took no oil with them; But the wise took oil in their vessels with their lamps. While the bridegroom tarried, they all slumbered and slept. And at midnight there was a cry made, Behold, the bridegroom cometh; go ye out to meet him. Then all those virgins arose, and trimmed their lamps. And the foolish said unto the wise, Give us of your oil; for our lamps are gone out. But the wise answered, saying, Not so; lest there be not enough for us and you; but go ye rather to them that sell, and buy for yourselves. And while they went to buy, the bridegroom came; and they that were ready went in with him to the marriage; and the door was shut. Afterward came also the other virgins, saying, Lord, Lord, open to us. But he answered and said, Verily I say unto you, I know you not. Watch therefore, for ye know neither the day nor the hour wherein the Son of man cometh. Matt. 25:1–13, KJV.

In the Near East, where the ancient customs are still practiced, the people do not pay attention to time as we do in the Western world. Therefore, a wedding feast may be set for six o'clock in the evening; but the feast may take place at midnight, three o'clock the next morning, or two to three days later than the original date that had been set. This is why Jesus commends the five virgins who were very wise and brought extra oil with them. But why did the virgins have to bring oil at all?

The majority of Eastern weddings normally take place in the early autumn or in the winter. Generally, a wedding feast will start in the evening and continue all night. The celebration for a rich man usually lasts seven days and seven nights; for a a poor man, three days and three nights. People use candles or oil lamps for their light. Butter is also used as fuel for their lamps. The reception house is generally lighted by the people bringing candles and lamps. When the bride and the bridegroom are fully prepared and are ready with the procession to enter the reception, only those with candles and lights may enter. No wedding is properly conducted without abundance of light.

Many visitors from nearby towns will also come to purchase the oil that is available, but then these visitors to their dismay may discover that the stores are closed and the oil vendors are waiting for the coming of the bride. Therefore, the wise virgins always carry extra oil should the bride and bridegroom be delayed.

Preparation for the festivities, especially the preparation of the bride and bridegroom, may take a long time. According to the ancient custom, the bride and bridegroom are bathed. There may be difficulties in procuring water, which would delay the wedding feast. The bride usually wears no less than seven dresses, and her face is totally veiled and hidden from the view of the people. Besides the "normal" delays that may occur, Easterners believe in taking plenty of time doing things.

The meaning of Jesus' parable is very clear; that is, Jesus' disciples, apostles and all followers were to be well prepared. They were to work for the goals of the kingdom of heaven. The apostles and followers could relate very easily to this parable. No doubt they had seen some of the young virgins refused entry into the reception house because of their lateness.

WEDDING AT CANA

John in his gospel reports a wedding feast that he attended with his master at Cana in Galilee. Mary, the mother of Jesus, was attending along with her son and a few of his disciples. "And when the wine ran low, his mother said to Jesus, They have no wine. Jesus said to her, What is it to me and to you, woman, my turn has not yet come. His mother said to the helpers, Whatever he tells you, do it." John 2:3-5, Lamsa translation. The King James Version reads somewhat differently. It says, "Jesus saith unto her, Woman, what have I to do with thee? mine hour is not yet come."

It appears as if Jesus had rebuked his mother, but this was not the case. It was in a very mild manner that Jesus spoke to his mother. Calling her, "woman," is a typical Aramaic, Semitic expression of politeness. The Aramaic term *AT-THA*, "woman," is spoken in the same sense as our English term "madame." The phrase, "My *hour* has not yet come," should be translated, "My *turn* has not yet come." The Aramaic word *SHAA* means "hour," "turn," and "time." In this particular passage it means "turn." Jesus refers to the custom of purchasing and providing wine at wedding feasts. What he says to his mother is, "Of what concern is it of ours? It is not my turn to buy wine."

One must understand the custom of entertaining at a feast. In the reception house men sit on the floor in a line according to their age and social status. The women usually sit on the opposite side, but in a circle. Near the door, servants usually stand by ready to attend the people. The musicians may also occupy a position near the door.

The bridegroom supplies all the food. However, some favorite foods are also brought in by neighbors as gifts to the couple. But the wine is provided by the guests. Each guest takes his turn in ordering the servants to procure wine. As the wine is being poured by the servant, he mentions the name of the guest who has purchased it. Then it is drunk by all to the health and happiness of the newlyweds. Every guest must do his duty in this matter so the wedding feast will be a success. However, each guest must be careful not to call to the servants to bring wine when it is not his turn. If this should happen, even by mistake, it would create resentment among other guests who had not had their turn. The guest who may have stepped out of turn from this traditional procedure would be regarded as ''an enemy.'' The reason for this is each guest must show his friendship and loyalty to the bridegroom by giving generously when it is time. If someone steps out of turn, it would be insulting to the guests who are of a higher social status.[9]

Jesus knew when it was his turn to serve the wine. And this is all that Jesus meant by telling his mother, ''My hour has not yet come.'' Mary realized her son was aware of the situation. She immediately informed the servants to be ready to serve wine when Jesus called for it. Mary also assured the helpers she would pay for the wine. In the East , when a mother and son travel together, the mother usually holds the family purse. Eastern robbers would consider it cowardly to steal from a woman.

THE LAST SUPPER

Most readers of the Bible visualize this momentous scene of the last supper in a totally Western setting, not realizing that they are being influenced by the famous painting of Leonardo da Vinci. This renowned Italian artist gave the world a beautiful character study in his painting of the last supper. However, we must understand that da Vinci was not portraying an historical Eastern setting. His entire work —the room, the table, the attire of the apostles and Jesus, and even the seating arrangements—are of his day and time. What we have in this painting is an Italian provincial scene and not one of the Near East.

The following description, then, is based on the typical Eastern customs observed at such a supper. Jesus and his disciples sat on the floor in a circle in one of the small rooms of a *BALAKHANA*, an inn for men only. The apostles and Jesus all wore hats during the supper. Spread on the floor in the center of the room was a cloth called in Aramaic *PATHORA*. Placed on the *PATHORA* were an earthen cup, a little jar filled with wine, and two or three large dishes. The cup was put in the center within reach of everyone in the circle. The jar was near Jesus.

According to eastern customs, on such occasions each of the few large plates contained a different kind of food. Bread is passed around. Meat is wrapped in thin loaves of bread, (this is called sop) put into pockets, and often carried home. The guests do not hesitate to reach for food on other men's dishes.

The posture of the beloved disciple, John, who was leaning on Jesus' chest, is also a common social custom. To this day, very close male friends still maintain this attitude while eating together, and it is as natural as shaking hands in the West. However, this show of affection is especially practiced when intimate friends are about to part from one another, as on the eve of a journey or when about to face a perilous assignment.

During this supper Jesus "let himself go;" that is, he expressed his feelings freely and openly to his disciples. He let them know of his disappointment in one who was about to betray him, and because these men would never meet in this manner again, he also made other statements which are commonly spoken at a "farewell supper."

The things Jesus said and did at the last supper were not isolated or uncommon events in the Semitic culture. A brotherly atmosphere and intimate, emotional expressions usually characterize a supper of this type among Eastern people, especially in the shadow of approaching danger.

It is the custom of a gracious host to ask for a joyous ending to a visit by having the whole company of men drink from one cup as a sign of their friendship. The phrase, "Do this in remembrance of me," is an affectionate request and means, "I love you; therefore I am always with you." When Jesus had made this request of his disciples they understood his loving statement to mean, "A powerful bond of love is between us, and because of this love we cannot be separated from one another."[10] In other words, he would no longer be with them.

At Eastern feasts, and especially in the region of Galilee, sharing food with those who stand and serve wine and water to the guests is common. However, exchanges of food with friends take on a deeper meaning. Choice portions of food are handed to friends as signs of close intimacy. This type of exchange is never done with an enemy.

Once again, Jesus let his feelings be revealed when he handed Judas, the betrayer, his "sop." "And when he (Jesus) had dipped the sop, he gave it to Judas Iscariot, the son of Simon." John 13:16. By understanding this Eastern custom, one quickly comprehends the act of love Jesus demonstrated by sharing his sop with Judas, for Jesus truly practiced his own teachings: "Love your enemies." In essence, he was telling Judas, through this sharing, that he did not in fact consider him an enemy. Jesus felt deep compassion and love for Judas, and with this symbolic gesture he was saying, "Here is my bread of friendship, and what you have to do, do it quickly."[11] Shortly thereafter Jesus was betrayed and sold to his priestly adversaries by Judas.

It was at this supper that Jesus sealed his love and friendship with his disciples. Pointing to the lamb and the bread and then to the wine, he said that his body was to become like the lamb and bread, broken and eaten; his blood was like the wine, drunk by all. He gave his life to reveal a new way of living for all mankind.

GIVING FOOD TO CHILDREN AT NIGHT

Another custom that Jesus makes reference to is the giving of food to children. In the King James Version of the Gospel of Luke 11:11-13, Jesus teaches and says:

> If a son shall ask bread of any of you that is a father will he give him a stone? Or if he ask a fish, will he for a fish give him a serpent? Or if he shall ask an egg, will he offer him a scorpion? If ye then, being evil, know how to give good gifts unto your children: how much more shall your heavenly Father give the Holy Spirit to them that ask him?

The Aramaic-Lamsa translation, reads:

> For who is among you, a father, if his son should ask him bread, what! would he hand him a stone? And if he should ask him a fish, what! would he hand him a snake instead of a fish? And if he should ask him for an egg, what! would he hand him a scorpion? So if you, who err, know how to give good gifts to your children, how much more will your father give the Holy Spirit from heaven to those who ask him?

In the East during the night a child may cry because he is hungry, and the father, giving him a fish or an egg, would be careful not to accidentally hand him a scorpion instead. An error like this can occur in the Near Eastern household because scorpions often crawl into the tents and are frequently found with the bread and eggs, or in the straw where the eggs are kept.

According to the King James Version of the Bible, Jesus

tells his listeners that they are evil, "If ye then, being evil, etc.," but as you can see, according to the Aramaic— Lamsa translation, this is not the case. Jesus said, "So if you, who err, etc." In other words, Jesus tells us that a father, being human, may err or make a mistake in giving a gift of bread to his child at night. The term "evil" in this particular scripture does not mean "evil" as we often think of it. It simply means an error or mistake. The word "evil," *BISHA*, also means immature and imperfect. What Jesus says in essence is, "if we who are human and make mistakes are still very discriminating and careful to give our children good gifts, how much more so is our heavenly Father discriminating and careful to give us only that which is beneficial to us."

This is the reason our heavenly Father gives us the Holy Spirit; but why would one need the Holy Spirit in obtaining appropriate gifts? The Holy Spirit—that is, the spirit of truth—which is in man, can guide him to the gifts that he is seeking; but sometimes one may ask for things which may be harmful to him or his family, for the human mind many times fails to see the whole picture. When one seeks the counsel of God in the things he or she undertakes, then good gifts will be the result of this seeking. When people are guided by the spirit, they are inspired to do that which is good, beneficial and without error. "For it is God who inspires you with the will to do the good things which you desire to do." Phil. 2:13, Lamsa translation.

COVERING THE HEAD

According to the ancient Eastern custom, women always kept their faces veiled, their heads covered in the presence of holy men, seers, priests, rabbis, or any religious authority, and men in general. The women veiled their faces not out of fear but out of reverence and respect. There are incidents in the Old Testament where this custom is mentioned. For instance, Rebekah covered herself when she saw Isaac coming to greet her as a token of respect to him. (Gen. 24:65). Women also had to cover their faces when praying. The apostle Paul mentions this custom in 1 Cor. 11:4–5, "Every man praying or prophesying, having his head covered, dishonoureth his head. But every woman that prayeth or prophesieth with her head uncovered dishonoreth her head: for that is even all one as if she were shaven." KJV.

The Aramaic text is clearer in the last part of verse 5: "and every woman who prays or phophesies with her head uncovered dishonors her head; for she is equal to her whose head is shaven." Lamsa translation.

In Eastern countries harlots were punished by having their heads shaved. Since the dignity and beauty of Eastern women were determined by the length of their hair, to have it cut or shaven would be disgraceful and would mean that these women were harlots. The apostle Paul recommends that the Christian Eastern women continue to abide by the old traditional customs of praying with their faces veiled and their heads covered. To do otherwise would be considered a shameful act, of course, in the eyes of Eastern men only. Jesus never taught obedience to the traditions of men when praying.

When Eastern men pray, they remove their hats and shoes as a sign of reverence to God. When men are condemned and are put to death, then their heads are covered. ". . . As the word went out of the king's mouth, they covered Haman's face." Esther 7:8. When the Sanhedrin council condemned Jesus for blasphemy, they covered his head as a sign that he had transgressed the holy law. "Then some of the men began to spit in his face and they covered his face and struck him on his head, saying 'Prophesy;' and the soldiers smote him on his cheeks." Mark 14.65.

The Length of Hair

According to Eastern traditional customs, a man must not have long hair because it would be considered a shame and a disgrace to him, but a woman having long hair signified great beauty and dignity. Even the Mosaic law prohibited men from having long hair. "You shall not let the hair of your heads grow, neither shall you trim the corners of your beard." Lev. 19:27. Once again, Paul in his letter to the Corinthians makes a comment about hair. "Does not even nature itself teach you that if a man have long hair, it is a disgrace to him? But if a woman have long hair, it is a glory to her; for her hair is given her for a covering. But if any man dispute these things, we have no precedent, neither has the church of God." 1 Cor. 11:14–16, Lamsa translation. "Does not even nature itself teach you that if a man have long hair, it is a disgrace to him?" This particular saying by Paul might be derived from a Jewish commentary. We know that primitive man kept his hair long to protect his body. The cutting of hair came later. Apparently men cut their hair to be distinguished from women, and the practice of cutting hair was probably instituted by some religious ordinance.

The term "nature" used by the apostle Paul might mean an ancient custom or manner which, after it is adopted, becomes "natural." In reality, nature has nothing to do with religious customs and manners, and nature "doesn't care" whether man's hair is long or short. However, it is traditional for men to be distinguished from women by the means of hair and clothes. All these customs came by adoption and have nothing to do with the teaching of Jesus. Customs and manners are changeable within each culture. The apostle Paul goes on to say that neither the apostles nor the church has any precedent on which to argue about hair. However in the Book of Judges, we read that Samson's long hair gave him power and glory and not disgrace. His parents were told by God that no razor was to touch his hair. When Samson broke this command, he lost power. There were many men in the Old Testament who took the Nazarite Vow and let the hair of their heads grow. Once the vow was completed, then the hair was cut. (See Numbers 6:1-8).

A few decades from now men and women may dress identically and custom may demand that they do so. Enlightenment and salvation does not depend on mere observances of customs, traditions and manners. The apostle Paul teaches that enlightenment and salvation come by the grace of God and the practical teachings of Jesus Christ.

CONCLUSION

There are numerous customs to explore throughout the entire Bible which would take many volumes to write about. However, for those of you who wish to pursue further studies of customs and manners, I would recommend that the reader consult the bibliography.

CHAPTER 5

The Fifth Key
Biblical Psychology

The customs and manners of a people are usually based on the traditional thinking and consciousness of that particular nation. Threfore, understanding the psychological makeup of the Near Eastern people, especially those of the biblical lands, is very important in the study of the Bible.

> Had the creed-makers of Christendom approached the Bible by way of Oriental psychology, had they viewed the Scriptures against the background of Syrian life, they would not have dealt with Holy Writ as a jurist deals with legislative enactments. Again, had the unfriendly critics of the Bible real acquaintance with the land of its birth, they would not have been so sure that the Bible was ''a mass of impossibilities.'' The sad fact is that the Bible has suffered violence from literalists among its friends, as from its enemies.[1]

When we thoughtfully consider the psychology of a people from a non-judgmental perspective, we will be able to comprehend a little more easily why they behave in a ''given manner'' or say things which may appear as ''strange'' to us. For instance, some of the teachings of Jesus have been branded by many critics as "contradictory," "impractical" and "irrelevant for today's world." The reason for this harsh criticism is that the psychological basis from which Jesus taught was not considered. We very easily may draw invalid conclusions from various biblical passages because we see them through our own eyes and not through the eyes of the Near East.

The fourth key, Eastern customs and manners, overlaps the fifth key. To a great extent, the culture and psychology are inseparable. Thus, we shall review the biblical customs and attitudes together. A word of reminder: the purpose of this writing is neither to condemn nor to condone any Eastern attitude, but the intent is to bring enlightenment to a particular verse or incident in the Bible.

TIME

Eastern people value friendships and relationships more highly than they do the observance of time. Family ties are very strong in the Near East. An Easterner does not give much attention to time, details, nor perfect accuracy in the things he says and does. In fact, many Westerners cannot fully comprehend when an Easterner may say something he does not mean at all; but, on the other hand, it is just as distressful for an Easterner to take notice of how many matters or things a Westerner may mean but does not say at all!

To an Easterner, the short, straight to the meaning expressions of Western people seem to drain from life its pleasures and to place a "disproportionate value on time." To the Eastern way of thinking, the major value of time must not be computed in terms of business and money, but rather in modes of sociability and rich, joyful companionship. A poetical sense of life and not prosaic accuracy must take precedence in living. In the Western world, describing events with utmost care and detail is very important, but to the Easterner it does not matter. He sees basically no difference between five o'clock and five-thirty or whether an event or conversation took place on a housetop or in the house. The main object is to know the substance of what had taken place with as many of the backup details as may be "conveniently remembered."[2]

Biblical authorities from the schools of criticism often scrutinize the Scriptures and find many discrepancies and inconsistencies. They find it baffling when the gospel writer says, "and after six days Jesus taketh Peter, James and John, his brother, and brought them up into a high mountain apart, and was transfigured before them: And his face did shine as the sun." These authorities want to know, "After six days from what time?" But throughout all four gospels there are many gaps and abrupt beginnings such as: "In those days," "Then came the disciples to Jesus," "And it came to pass," "When Jesus came into the coast of Caesarea Philippi," and many other similar expressions which seem to point nowhere and have no continuity or relatedness to the passage before it or after it. Therefore the gospels appear to us as rather inconsistent. In order to clarify the "inconsistenceies," we need to understand how the gospel writer thought and expressed himself. He had a total indifference to the minute details upon which we in the West place so much emphasis. The Eastern author was only interested in *what* Jesus *did* and *what* he *said*. *Where* it was said *when* it was said might differ with each scribe. We look upon that with great horror and mistrust, but to an Easterner this represents no difficulty at all.

Another very good example of not taking an Easterner literally when he mentions time is when Jesus said, "For as Jonah was in the whale's belly three days and three nights, so the Son of man will be in the heart of the earth three days and three nights." Matt. 12:40, KJV. But was Jesus in the heart of the earth for exactly three days and three nights? According to the scriptures he was crucified on Friday afternoon and taken down from the cross before the sabbath, that is, sunset. He was placed in a borrowed tomb Friday evening. He lay in the tomb all Friday night, all day Saturday, but he arose from the sepulcher early Sunday morning. That does not constitute a literal three days and three nights. But to an Easterner it does. It was Friday, Saturday and Sunday.

Even to this day, if you were to visit an Eastern friend who lived his life according to the old habits of thinking and you remained one day with him, he would tell everyone that you had been with him for three days and three nights. We, of course, think of this as a lie, but to an Easterner that much detail does not matter. Most of the inconsistencies and discrepancies found in the recordings of the gospel, as I stated earlier, do not represent a problem to the Eastern mind, but they do to the Western mind. Had the learned authorities realized the habits and psychological makeup of the Eastern people, perhaps it would have saved them from doubting so much of what they read in the Scriptures and from "over-criticizing" the validity of the Bible.

WOMEN

Probably on no other topic do the Eastern and Western worlds differ more extensively than on the status of women. As I mentioned earlier, my purpose is not to judge Near Eastern attitudes about anything, especially concerning women. Nor is it my place to condemn or condone, neither accuse nor excuse, these particular attitudes. But the purpose of this book is merely to describe the psychological basis and the customs involving women of the Near East and to relate them to the biblical setting in which they come to us. Basically, the attitude towards women in the

East is misunderstood by Western peoples. The unwritten social code which dominates the Near Eastern culture gives men the precedence. The Near Eastern culture is a male oriented society. Easterners feel it is "unnecessary and uncomplimentary to both sexes to give women social and domestic prominence." Eastern people also feel that the "Western man has become the slave of his wife." All this amounts to a serious misunderstanding on the part of both worlds to see the fine grass roots of each culture.

Enough said in regard to the differences between the East and the West. Let us now consider the purpose of this key, which is to clarify different passages of the Bible.

What Paul Really Said About Women

Some Bible readers and teachers think that the things the apostle Paul said about women were not translated correctly. Therefore, a misconception prevails in our minds. Again, in order to understand the writings of Paul, one must consider the social customs and psychology of the people. When we understand the Scripture in its sociological and psychological setting, all misconceptions will be clarified.

Paul in his letter to the Corinthians states the old traditional Near Eastern attitude:

see next page

For a man indeed ought not to cover his head, forasmuch as he is the image and glory of God: but the woman is the glory of the man. For the man is not of the woman; but the woman of the man. Neither was the man created for the woman; but the woman for the man. For this cause ought the woman to have power on her head because of the angels. Nevertheless neither is the man without the woman, neither the woman without the man, in the Lord. For as the woman is of the man, even so is the man also by the woman; but all things of God. 1 Cor. 11:7–12, KJV.

The Lamsa translation of the Aramaic text reads:

> For a man indeed ought not cover his head, because he is the image and glory of God; but the woman is the glory of the man. For the man was not created from the woman; but the woman was created from the man. Neither was the man created for the woman; but the woman for the man. For this reason the woman ought to be modest and cover her head as a mark of respect to the angels. Nevertheless, in our Lord (according to what Jesus taught us) there is no preference between man and woman, neither between woman and man. For as the woman is of the man, even so is the man also by the woman; but all things of God.

As we can readily see, the English translation of the Aramaic text is very clear. The apostle merely restates the people's position and belief system of the time. But then he says, "Nevertheless, in our Lord, that is, according to what Jesus taught us, *there is no preference between man and woman,* neither between woman and man." He states his case very clearly. Paul transcends the religious social custom and belief of his day. He was able to do this because he knew the teaching of Jesus. Jesus taught the original concept of man and woman: They both are the image and likeness of God. One is not inferior. Neither is the other superior, but both are God's likeness.

Jesus taught directly from Genesis 1:27, which says, "So God made man in his image and likeness; male and female made he them." Therefore, both are in essence spiritual beings.

The true status of women, according to the author of Genesis, Chapter 1, is equality with men spiritually. But what did Paul mean when he said, "For this reason the woman ought to be modest and cover her head as a mark of respect to the angels"? In the Near East women always cover their faces in the presence of holy men, not as a sign of fear but out of respect, dignity and reverence. All kind, pious and good-hearted men and women are addressed as "angels of God." Easterners also believe that when they pray, angels are present to take their supplications before the throne of God. In this particular instance, the term "angels" means holy or pious men. Interestingly, Jesus did not teach man-made Jewish ordinances and racial customs. He knew men and women were equal and said nothing about women covering their heads.

WOMEN KEEP SILENT

To this very day Eastern women remain silent and do not participate orally in worship services. They stand behind the congregation of men and observe with great appreciation the duties which the men perform.

In the temple or mosque of the orthodox Jewish and Islamic faiths women have their own separate places of worship. Generally, many pious women do not attend services but pray and study the scriptures at home. They also learn from their husbands, brothers, sons, and the priests and teachers of their particular religions. The apostle Paul understood very well the tenacious hold the ancient traditional Semitic customs held on the society of his day. It would have been scandalous to allow a woman to stand before a congregation of men and read the Scriptures. She would have to unveil her face in order to read. Such an act would disrupt the services. Men would be looking at the woman instead of listening to what was being read. This is why Paul says again in his letter to Timothy, "Let the woman learn in silence with all subjection. But I suffer not a woman to teach, nor to usurp authority over the man, but to be in silence." 1 Tim. 2:11-12, KJV.

None of these customs, however, are based on Jesus' teachings. Jesus did not exclude women. He did not uphold some of the old customs or beliefs which discriminated against women. However, the apostle Paul did uphold the custom of women not speaking, singing or participating in any way in the service. He knew that Eastern men could not bear at that time the problems women's freedom would create in the services and in that society. But as one carefully searches through the scriptures we find Miriam, the sister of Moses and Aaron, and other women singing and praising God with timbrels. (See Ex. 15:20-21). And according to some of the biblical New Testament records, women were always supporters of the faith. They definitely played a role, and a very important one, in the spread of their faith.

OBEDIENCE

Wives, submit yourselves to your husbands as to our Lord. For the husband is the head of the wife, even as Christ is the head of the church, and he is the saviour of the body. Therefore as the church is subject to Christ, so let the wives be to their own husbands in every thing. Husbands, love your wives, even as Christ loved his church and gave himself for it." Eph. 5:22-25, KJV.

Women are not permitted to transact business or engage in teaching or minister in spiritual work outside of the home. Women look to their husbands for advice, support and security. The husband, however, can carry on business negotiations without ever consulting his wife. In the Near East a husband is an overlord, but, even in spite of this, at certain times and in certain cases where women have a better business judgment than the husbands, the wives will interfere and conduct business. In these cases the women must be courageous when they take things into their own hands and try to guide their spouses, which may result in family quarrels.

Evidently among the people at Ephesus, that is, the Christian converts, there was some discontent among the married couples, and Paul instructs them to work in love and in harmony. He recommends that the wives should be obedient to their husbands in matters which concern the family affairs in general and that they conduct their lives with mutual understanding and love. He does not mean that women should submit themselves to cruelty or mistreatment.

Among some Eastern faiths, and even in the Moslem religion, women have restricted freedom and can say very little. However, in the teachings of Jesus a husband and wife are one just as the head and the body are one. Paul always recommends love and loyalty to be the tie that binds the husband and wife. Jesus knew and understood the conditions under which women lived in the Near East. This is why he was so protective of women in regard to divorce.

DIVORCE AND REMARRIAGE

According to the King James Version of the Bible Jesus is reported to have said:

> It hath been said, Whosoever shall put away his wife, let him give her a writing of divorcement: But I say unto you, that whosoever shall put away his wife, saving for the cause of fornication, causeth her to commit adultery: and whosoever shall marry her that is divorced committeth adultery. Matt. 5:31–32.

But according to the Lamsa translation based on the Aramaic text, Jesus is reported to have said:

> It has been said that whoever divorces his wife, must give her the divorce papers. But I say to you that whoever divorces his wife, except for fornication, causes her to commit adultery; and whoever marries a woman who is separated but not divorced, commits adultery. Matt. 5:31–32.

According to the Eastern text a divorced woman is permitted to remarry providing she is divorced and not just separated. Marriage, according to Eastern belief, is a sacred institution. Therefore, nearly all Easterners feel that marriage should not be mixed with politics or courts as is the case in our Western world. Civil marriages are not practiced nor recognized. What is necessary is a payment of dowry and the blessings pronounced by a priest or rabbi. Only these matters form the sacred bond between a man and his wife in the East. When a marriage is arranged the woman's consent is not considered. Therefore, women have nothing to say when the question of divorce arises. The sole power is invested in the man who exercises unlimited authority over his wife or wives. Among the Assyrian Christians of the Near East who still follow the old biblical laws, there are very few cases of divorce, and the attitude of the men towards their wives differs considerably from other Semitic races. They are usually more liberal, and to some degree, the women exercise certain freedoms equal to that of women of the Western world. According to the present-day law among these descendants of the ancient Assyrian people, if a man marries a woman who has been abandoned and not divorced, both the man and the woman are excommunicated from the church; but, if a woman who has been abandoned by her husband obtains divorce papers, she is allowed to remarry and this is considered lawful.

A clearer understanding concerning the divorce question can be gained by studying the divorce customs among non-Christian Semites such as the Jews in Mesopotamia and Persia, the Arabians, and the non-Semitic races who are influenced by Semitic religion and culture as the Kurds and Persians. They are still fully governed by the ancient Biblical law. Some of these people divorce their wives for no criminal or moral reason but for other causes which are regarded as justifying divorce. Among these causes are not bearing children, not working hard, not having found favor in a husband's eyes, looking at other men. If any interference should come from religious authorities, a small bribe of a lamb, a chicken, or two pounds of sugar, would be sufficient to appease these authorities and obtain their consent. For unknown ages, Eastern women have been degraded and regarded as man's property, at times even bought and sold in open markets. Divorces are so easy and frequent that religious laws have been instituted to remedy the situation.[5]

Jesus condemned the abandonment of wives by their husbands for any arbitrary reason. He did not approve of the lax laws which favored Eastern men. Hence, Jesus' consideration about divorce was very strict in order to protect Eastern women from being put out in the streets. He definitely championed the rights of women and gave them equality with men. This is also the reason that the apostle Paul in his letters states that in Christ, i.e., through the teachings of Jesus, there is neither male nor female. This discrimination was to end through the powerful gospel of Jesus.

Eastern Laws

Because of the ease with which one may divorce in the Near East, certain laws were instituted to make divorce more difficult, and thus an attempt was made to relieve the situation. For instance, legislation had been enacted which stated that if a man divorced his wife for no reason and then realized that he had made a mistake and wanted her back, the woman first had to marry another man and live with him for two or three months. When that period of time had passed, the formerly divorced wife could then obtain a divorce paper so that she could remarry her first husband. This was based on the Koranic law. Men of Islamic faith are not so quick to divorce their wives knowing that they must give their wives in marriage to a new husband. This is embarrassing and extremely humiliating. However in Kurdistan, among the Kurds who are also members of the Islamic faith, if any one of them should divorce his wife and then later desire to remarry her, the woman is immediately married to a goat or to an ox. Then after the marriage, the unfortunate ox or goat is killed and the woman goes into mourning since she has now become a widow. When that time of mourning is past, she is then permitted to remarry her former husband.[6]

Jesus' Teachings

In the section of the Bible that we call "The Sermon on the Mount," Jesus taught many things based on Eastern psychology. For example, "Ye have heard that it hath been said, An eye for an eye, and a tooth for a tooth; But I say unto you, That ye resist not evil; but whosoever shall smite thee on thy right cheek, turn to him the other also." Matt. 5:38–39, KJV.

Resisting evil only increases the power of evil. The Aramaic idiom and expression, "to turn the other cheek," means "learn to take the wind out of the other person's sails," or "do not augment a problem." In English we would say "nip it in the bud." In other words, don't retaliate! It will only encourage more drastic reprisals. The psychology behind this teaching is to weaken and lessen the ''evil'' force that may come against you. How? By not resisting the evil, it cannot escalate. For instance, if one should say something provocative to another and thus anger him to strike back with force, then a fight might ensue. Better to turn the other cheek.

''And if any man will sue thee at the law, and take away thy coat, let him have thy cloak also.'' Matt. 5:40, KJV. Small-time thieves generally steal garments and shoes. Clothes are stolen from homes and fields as well. Also according to the ancient custom, when a man is taken to court under suspicion, his garments are generally taken as a bond. Sometimes innocent men are accused of being bandits and are brought before the officials. If the man is found guilty and has no financial means to help himself, then his apparel will be confiscated. Clothes are also accepted as collateral for loans. When individuals fail to make their payments, creditors are also willing to accept clothing in lieu of payment. If at any time a man should resist giving his robe, he will not only be forced to give up his robe and shirt, but many other garments will be taken by force and the man will be severely punished.[7]

Jesus meant that it is better to surrender your shirt and your robe than to lose everything. According to the ancient custom, Easterners wear at one time many shirts and robes, one upon another, in summer and winter. According to the late Dr. George Lamsa, he states, ''A man generally wears all the garments he owns because in the East his social standing is determined by the number of clothes he wears.''[8] Once again, the psychological principle of non-resistance is taught. When we resist an evil, we compound the ''evil,'' the injustice. Jesus does not mean one must take unnecessary abuse and allow others to totally disregard his rights.

''Whoever compels you to carry a burden for a mile, go

with him two." Jesus reemphasizes his principle of not resisting an injustice. In the ancient days of the Near East and also in some areas of the Near East today where modern modes of transportation were and are unknown, food supplies and materials are usually carried on the backs of animals and men; and at times men and women must carry wheat and other foods at least fifteen to twenty-five miles or more. Many times military supplies are carried by men and animals from one town to another; that is, the townsfolk of one city carried the supplies to another city, and then new recruits are selected from the new town. Those men and women who do not resist but willingly carry the supplies are released as soon as possible or even at the next town. But those men and women who resist being recruited and refuse to carry anything, are forced to carry burdens for three days or more. Besides, they may also be beaten. The willingness to go more than a mile may open an opportunity for an individual not to go any miles at all, or at least a short distance.[9]

LOVING ONE'S ENEMY

> Ye have heard that it hath been said, Thou shalt love thy neighbor, and hate thine enemy. But I say unto you, Love your enemies, bless them that curse you, do good to them that hate you, and pray for them which despitefully use you, and persecute you; That ye may be the children of your Father which is in heaven; for he maketh his sun to rise on the evil and on the good, and sendeth rain on the just and on the unjust. Matt. 5:43–45, KJV.

When an Easterner has an enemy, he believes his enemy is also the enemy of God. In the Old Testament the enemies of Israel were considerd the enemies of the God of Israel.

When an Easterner hates an enemy he brings down curses upon his enemy's head, all in the name of God. Here is an example of this kind of thinking:

> Hold not thy peace, O God of my praise; For the mouth of the wicked and the mouth of the deceitful are opened against me; . . . And they have rewarded me evil for good, and hatred for my love. Set thou a wicked man over him; and let Satan stand at his right hand. (Let them be ill-advised.) When he shall be judged, let him be condemned; and let his prayer become sin. Let his days be few; and let another take his office. Let his children be fatherless, and his wife a widow. Let his children be continually vagabonds, and beg; let them seek their bread also out of their desolate places. Let the extortioner catch all that he hath; and let the strangers spoil his labour. Let there be none to extend mercy unto him; neither let there be any to favour his fatherless children. Let his posterity be cut off; and in the generation following let their name be blotted out. Let them be before the Lord continually, that he may cut off the memory of them from the earth. Because that he remembered not to shew mercy, but persecuted the poor and needy man, that he might even slay the broken in heart. And as he loved cursing, so let it come unto him as he delighted not in blessing, so let it be far from him. Psalm 109: 1–17, KJV.

One can readily see what Jesus meant when he said, "Bless anyone who curses you." It is difficult for us to understand how such a psalm could be present in the Scriptures. But, here again we need to consider Eastern temperament:

> If you will keep in mind the juvenile temperament of the Oriental, already mentioned, and his habit of

turning to God in all circumstances, as unreservedly as a child turns to his father, your judgment of the son of Palestine will be greatly tempered with mercy.

The one redeeming feature in these imprecatory petitions is that they have always served the Oriental as a safety valve. Much of his wrath is vented in this manner. He is much more cruel in his word than in his deeds. As a rule the Orientals quarrel much, but fight little. By the time two antagonists have cursed and reviled each other so profusely they cool off, and thus graver consequences are averted. The Anglo-Saxon has outgrown such habits. In the first place the highly complex social order in which he lives calls for much more effective methods for the settling of disputes, and, in the second place, he has no time to waste on mere words. And just as the Anglo-Saxon smiles at the wordy fights of the Oriental, the Oriental shudders at the swiftness of the Anglo-Saxon using his fists and his pistol. Both are needy of the grace of God.[10]

Jesus encourages his countrymen to love their enemies and bless those who may curse them. This statement by Jesus is the very core of his dynamic principles. Jesus knew that only the powerful energy of love can truly disarm and dispel a so-called enemy. When one loves an enemy he has no enemy. One cannot legislate a man to love an enemy, but Jesus knew that only love from each individual soul could heal hatreds and resentments. Each individual must look to his own soul and find the wellspring of love which is resident within his being. This is what we call "God." No wonder Jesus said that God lets his sun shine on the good and the bad and the rain fall on the just and the unjust. One does not know his capacity to love until he finds himself in a situation that calls for the depths of love from his own soul.

CHAPTER 6

The Sixth Key
Biblical Symbolism

The sixth key, symbolism, has three categories: parables, metaphors and poetical philosophy. The Semitic languages of Aramaic and Hebrew are very visual and symbolic. The alphabet, twenty-two letters, was originally twenty-two pictures. Each letter developed from a picture form. The letter "A" represents God. The Assyrians worshipped the ox, so therefore when they formed the letter "A" they drew an ox head. The letter "B" or *BETH*, means house, home and family. The letter "C" means food, transportation. The use of the language itself is very flowery and picturesque and, therefore, highly symbolic. Let us look into the first category under symbolism: Parables.

PARABLES

"All these things spake Jesus unto the multitude in parables; and without a parable spake he not unto them." Matt. 13:34, KJV.

The Aramaic word *PELATHA* means "parables," "proverbs," "allegories," and "illustrations." An Easterner makes

95

"no distinction between a proverb and a parable."[1] Teaching and carrying on a conversation in parables, proverbs, and illustrations is very characteristic of these people. Wise men, wazirs, court officials, rabbis, prophets, teachers and politicians always make use of parables in their debates and lectures. Merchants and clients, while bargaining, often mention a few parables. Eastern poets and musicians sing parables, proverbs and riddles as they play their musical instruments. In Psalm 49, verse 4, we read, "I will incline my ear to parables; I will sing my proverbs upon the harp." (Aramaic text). Telling parables was a common way of communicating among Easterners and remains so to this very day. Illustrated speech is very precious to them and is enjoyed by all. To the Eastern mind it is poetical, mystical and very social.

A parable is verbal imagery which portrays and illustrates an event or a teaching. The main purpose of a parable is to convey an impression, and not to construct definitions or to establish dogmas.[2] Parables were also spoken by Eastern teachers to test the listeners and to study their reaction to the stories. This was the case with the prophet Nathan who had to expose King David for committing adultery and murder. (See 2 Samuel 12:1–7).

A skilled Eastern orator or teacher uses many parables to illustrate the same point, repeating his lesson over and over again until he is absolutely certain his words have made an indelible impression on the minds of his students or listeners. The Aramaic and Hebrew style of writing and speaking is very intensive, colorful, descriptive and imaginative. These speakers are outstanding storytellers, holding their listeners to the last detail. Since imparting spiritual ideas and being entertaining at the same time was an art welcomed by the people, Jesus, no doubt, held his hearers spellbound with his parables. Surely Jesus was that very kind of speaker, a true son of the East. ". . . and without parables he did not speak to them."

The common folk of Jesus' day were not taught about the loving nature of God, nor did they readily understand the spiritual aspects of the kingdom of heaven and the coming messianic rule. They were taught that God would have nothing to do with sinners and that he dwelt in the heavens far above them and could only be appeased through sacrificial offerings. Even the religious teachers of that time did not fully grasp the spiritual significance of the kingdom. They thought the messianic kingdom was to be a political domain, ruled by God and enforced through the military might and power of the Messiah—the Christ. This materialistic viewpoint of the kingdom came about because of the literal and traditional interpretations of the holy Scriptures and because there were many conflicting interests in Judaism at that time. Some factions looked for political liberation, and others were satisfied with their present conditions under Herod's leadership. The teachings of the elders also helped to obscure the inner, spiritual meaning of the Scripture.

Jesus spoke in parables in order to clarify the different aspects of the kingdom of heaven and to change the prevailing theological concepts about God and the messianic kingdom. For example, it had been taught that the kingdom would come suddenly, in a twinkle of an eye, but Jesus understood that the kingdom would not manifest instantaneously. So he composed several parables to illustrate the idea that the kingdom of heaven would come gradually, and only as the living word rooted itself in the hearts and minds of the people and their leaders. He knew that an inner revolution of the heart and mind must take place for the kingdom to be established.

The parables that teach these ideas are: that of the sower, (the parable of the seed in Aramaic) Matt. 13:3–9; the parable of the mustard seed, Matt. 13:31–32, and the parable of the leaven, Matt. 13:33. Jesus also understood that men would have to search diligently and "sell out" completely for the truth—thus, the parable of the pearl of great price, Matt. 13:45-46. Then he gave three more parables which illustrate the loving care and concern of God for all men, even those who had lost their way. These are the lost sheep, the lost coin and the lost son, Luke 15:1-32.

A Misunderstanding

"And the disciples came, and said unto him, Why speakest thou unto them in parables? He answered and said unto them, Because it is given unto you to know the mysteries of the kingdom of heaven, but to them it is not given." Matt. 13:10-11, KJV.

I believe many students and interpreters of the Bible unintentionally misconstrue this statement of Jesus, since it is often understood to mean that Jesus spoke in parables to hide the "truth" of his teaching. Some even suggest that Jesus didn't want the common people to know the secret of the kingdom and that his teachings were for a "select" group. But, as has been stated earlier, parables were the common means of communication in the East. The main purpose of a parable was "to convey an impression and not to construct definitions or to establish dogmas." An Eastern teacher used many parables to illustrate the same point.

When Jesus' disciples wondered why their master didn't explain the mysteries of the kingdom to others in the same manner that he taught them, his reply was, ". . . to you it is given to know . . . but it is not given to them." This is where most interpreters misunderstand what Jesus said. To help make it plainer, I will paraphrase the words of Jesus, and the explanation would read like this: "You hear my teachings every day because you travel with me and remain at my side. You may ask any question you like, so you may be able to understand the secret of the kingdom. But I am with the crowds only a short time, and some of them will not hear me again. So I teach them in a way they can understand and remember and that is through my parables."

The simple people to whom Jesus spoke were victims of the false teachings and interpretations of the Pharisees, Sadducees, elders and scribes. The masses were not as fortunate as his disicples who could see and hear him continually. This is the reason Jesus told his disciples, "But as for you, blessed are your eyes, for they see; and your ears, for they hear. For truly I say to you, a great many prophets and righteous men have longed to see what you see, and did not see it; and to hear what you hear, and did not hear it."

Jesus' parables were simple and direct. From the very start of his ministry, he always endeavored to explain the mystery of the kingdom of heaven and to reveal the inner truth which was hidden from the hearts and minds of the people and the religious authorities.

ADAM AND EVE

The story of Adam and Eve, found in the second and third chapters of the Book of Genesis, is a parable. The parable itself also contains metaphors, figurative speech, which we in the Western world and so many of our Christian teachers have taken literally. (Interestingly, the term "garden" in Semitic languages also means "a wife.") Regardless of how one interprets this story, it is best understood when one realizes that this is a parable. God did not create a tree and say not to touch it. God, who is all powerful and all knowing, would not need to tempt man in order to learn how man would behave.

How does one know or how can one prove that the account of Adam and Eve is a parable? This is easily done because of the style in which it is written. According to the story, after Adam and Eve had transgressed and eaten of the tree of the knowledge of good and evil, God came in the

cool of the evening looking for them. As the Lord God passed through the garden he kept calling to them, "Adam,
where are you? Adam, where are you?" How could God,
who is omniscient, omnipotent and omnipresent, not
know where Adam and Eve were? Jesus said that God even
knows when a sparrow falls and knows the number of hairs
on our heads. And yet the Lord God did not know where
Adam and Eve were?

The author of this parable tells us that the Lord God was
also surprised to learn that Adam and Eve had been eating
of the tree that they had been forbidden to touch. "And the
Lord God said to Adam, Who told you that you were naked?
Have you eaten of the tree of which I commanded you that
you should not eat?" Adam, not willing to take the responsibility for his act, replies to the Lord God, "The *woman*
whom *thou gavest* to be with me, she gave me of the fruit
of the tree, and I did eat." Adam not only blamed Eve but
also the Lord God for having given to him that woman.
And when the Lord God turned to the woman she replied.
"The serpent beguiled me, and I did eat." Then the Lord
God takes up a conversation with the snake and says," Because you have done this thing, cursed are you above cattle,
and above all beasts of the field; on your belly shall you go,
and dust shall you eat all the days of your life."

If a reader accepts this record to be a literal event, it appears rather ridiculous for an omnipotent, omniscient and
omnipresent God to behave in such a manner. What we
must realize is that the author of the story casts God in four
major roles: As the owner of the garden, as a potter who
molded man from clay, as a surgeon who performed an ope-
ration on Adam and removed his rib to create a woman, and
finally as a tailor who sewed coats of skin for Adam and Eve
after their transgression and expulsion from the garden of
Eden. This is how we know the story is a parable. To take it
otherwise would mean that God is totally limited even as a
man is limited in his knowing.

Interestingly, Judaism never has taught and still does not teach, the Adam and Eve story in the light of "Original Sin" or as "The Fall of Man" in the sense of humanity as a whole. In fact the doctrine of "Original Sin" during the Middle Ages helped to instigate an unbelievable vilification of woman. It made her the authoress of death and all earthly woe. Judaism, instead of teaching the Fall of Man, teaches the Rise of Man; and instead of Original sin, it stresses Original Virtue, the beneficent hereditary influence of righteous ancestors upon their descendants. It also teaches that all the children of men are destined to help in the establishment of the kingdom of God on earth.[3] Also some Christian Bible teachers call attention to the fact that Jesus never refers to Original Sin or to the so-called Fall of Man in the gospels. But instead the Christ encouraged his followers to become like children so that they might enter the kingdom of heaven. If children are "born in sin," why would Jesus teach his disciples to become like children?

THE PROPHET HOSEA

Did the Lord God of Israel instruct the prophet Hosea to take a "wife of whoredoms"? Then a second time command him to take an adulterous woman for a wife? According to the book of Hosea, the Lord God did command the prophet to marry an adulteress and a harlot. But what was written by Hosea is not an historical event; it was a parable composed by the Hebrew seer. Hosea, through his parable, describes Israel and Judah as harlots who had abandoned the law of Moses, the Lord God and had made alliances with foreign nations. Prostitution was forbidden by the Mosaic law and harlots were stoned. Hosea, being a prophet of God, could not have bought a harlot and taken her as a wife, but he could do this in a parable, and it was understood as a parable.[4]

Through the use of metaphors and allegories, the prophet was able to demonstrate that both Israel and Judah had departed from the Lord God and the true religion of their forefathers. They were doomed to destruction by the very same nations upon whom they relied for safety and security. Israel's and Judah's unfaithfulness to the principles of their forefathers and the Mosaic law is depicted in a very graphic manner, so that even the uneducated farmer, shepherd, fisherman and country people could understand the predicament in which the two States were caught.

Figurative Speech

Easterners use metaphors extensively in their everyday speech. The use of metaphors, by no means, is limited to Eastern languages alone. However, it is more widely used by Easterners than by Westerners. We especially find this true in the biblical communication. Often in the Scriptures, great noblemen are pictured as trees and as the cedars of Lebanon. Nations are symbolized as animals. Imperial nations are depicted as lions, bears, and leopards. Smaller, weaker nations are pictured as lambs, sheep and goats. Metaphysically, different states of consciousness are also depicted as trees of life or the tree of the knowledge of good and evil. The last book of the New Testament, Revelation, is totally symbolic and must not be understood literally. For instance, it is written that John saw the Holy City, New Jerusalem, coming down from God, prepared as a bride adorned for her husband. The Holy City is a symbol and therefore should not be thought of as a structural city coming down from God out of the sky. (See Rev. 21:1-2) Prophetically and symbolically it represents a clear, caring state of mind which mankind is capable of expressing and will demonstrate universally in the future. The city also denotes a community of true believers who carry out justice, mercy and love for mankind.

Unfortunately, the use of figurative speech by biblical authors and prophets has unintentionally created some mistaken, invalid ideas in the Western mind about many Bible subjects. One of these subjects is a so-called supernatural being known as Lucifer.

THE ORIGIN OF LUCIFER

The following is not to be understood as a complete comprehensive work on the many references in the Bible made to the devil, satan, etc., but it is a brief study on the origin of Lucifer only. Haven't you often asked yourself these questions? . . . Has a loving God created a maleficent being who tempts us into doing evil? Is mankind plagued by a sinister power that rivals omnipotent God? Where did the name Lucifer originate and does he lure people away from truth and justice? Does the Bible actually make references to this evil personage and his fallen collaborators, therefore seeming to substantiate the existence of Lucifer?

We are told by certain interpreters of the Bible that God created Lucifer. However, there is absolutely no scripture that states that God created a supernatural being that turned on Him and is at present tempting and tormenting the inhabitants of earth. Then again, some Bible teachers claim that Lucifer definitely has a history and it is told in this manner: There was a rebellion in heaven. Lucifer, the light being, had persuaded a third of the angels to join forces with him and fight against God. This heavenly traitor desired to usurp the celestial throne and make himself God. Now according to what is told, God reacted to the uprising somewhat the way humans would react and handle such a threatening situation. The Almighty mobilized his good angels, and commanded Michael, the archangel, to do battle against the dissident horde. War began in heaven. Michael quickly defeated Lucifer and cast him and his angels out of heaven. But alas, this rebellious horde fell to the unfortunate earth. And now that great heavenly war is waged on earth.

The origin of Lucifer, the basic story of satan, is drawn from three major passages of the Bible: Isaiah 14:12–16, Ezekiel, 28:12–17, and Revelation 12:7–12. There is also a fourth passage which seems to confirm the first three passages: 2 Peter 2:4. Let us examine these famous portions of the Bible.

> How art thou fallen from heaven, O Lucifer, son of the morning! How art thou cut down to the ground, which didst weaken the nations! For thou hast said in thine heart, I will ascend into heaven, I will exalt my throne above the stars of God: I will sit also upon the mount of the congregation, in the sides of the north: I will ascend above the heights of the clouds; I will be like the most High. Yet thou shalt be brought down to hell, to the sides of the pit. They that see thee shall narrowly look upon thee, saying, is this the man that made the earth to tremble, that did shake kingdoms; Isaiah 14:12–16, KJV.

All these verses seem to be describing an unearthly event, but what does Isaiah say directly about his own prophetic proverb? In verse 4 of chapter 14, Isaiah is commanded to, ''Take up this proverb against *the king of Babylon* and say, How hath the oppressor ceased! The golden city ceased!'' The prophetic statesman knew about whom he spoke and it concerned the king of Babylon and *not* an angelic being and supernatural force. Furthermore, Isaiah uses descriptive Near Eastern metaphors in proclaiming the demise of the Babylonian Empire and its exalted leader and king. Before we look into the metaphorical meaning of these verses, let us see what the name ''Lucifer'' means.

The term ''Lucifer'' comes from the Hebrew word *HELEL* and literally means ''the shining one.'' It may also be translated "day star" or "morning star." Isaiah represents Nebuchadnezzar's days of power and glory metaphorically as "the morning star." The prophet contrasts the king's former pride and splendor with his grievous fall and degradation.

However, the Eastern Aramaic text offers us a different rendering of Isaiah's words: "How are you fallen from heaven! *Howl in the morning!* For you have fallen down to the ground, O reviler of the nations." (Isa. 14:12) The Aramaic word *AELEL* means "to shout," "cry out," and "howl." thus the term "Lucifer" is not present in the original Aramaic manuscripts.

The abundant use of metaphors is what makes a language colorful and especially so to an Easterner:

> Just as the Easterner loves to flavor his food strongly and to dress in bright colors, so is he fond of metaphor, exaggeration, and positiveness in speech . . .
> I could wish, however, that the learned theologians had suspected more strongly the literal accuracy of Eastern utterances and had thus been saved from founding a huge doctrinal structure on a figure of speech.[5]

One of the many bridges we must cross in attempting to understand the Bible is the extensive use of metaphors by its writers. And in our study of the origin of Lucifer we must realize that the prophets employed idiomatic, symbolic, and metaphorical terms of speech in expressing their ideas and messages to the common people of the East.

In describing the fall of the Babylonian monarch, the prophet Isaiah uses metaphors to depict Nebuchadnezzar's loss of power and glory. "How you are fallen from heaven!" cries the seer. But remember, Isaiah is not describing the fall of an angelic being, because "to fall from heaven" is a Semitic idiom and means an individual has "lost his power and influence." It is also understood in the East that when a star falls from heaven, it means a ruler, leader, or potentate has lost his authority or kingdom. (The book of Revelation makes many references to falling stars, which indicate political and governmental changes . . . usually the collapse of leadership.)

The Semitic expressions, "I will ascend into heaven, I will exalt my throne above the stars of God . . . I will ascend above the heights of the clouds, I will be like the most High," etc., are Eastern forms of exaggerated speech used to describe the glory, power and influence of an imperial ruler. In other words, the king's rule is so great that he will ascend into heaven. His throne is so high that it sits above the stars of God and the heights of the clouds. His reign is so powerful he is like the most High. But alas, the prophet predicts the king will be brought down to *SHEOL*, i.e., he is doomed to failure and will go the way of all flesh.

The second major scriptural passage employed by some theologians to substantiate the existence of Lucifer is found in Ezekiel 28:12-17.

> Son of man, take up a lamentation upon the king of Tyrus and say unto him, Thus saith the Lord God; Thou sealest up the sum, full of wisdom, and perfect in beauty. Thou hast been in Eden the garden of God; every precious stone was thy covering, the sardius, topaz, and the diamond, the beryl, the onyx and the jasper, the sapphire, the emerald, and the carbuncle, and gold; the workmanship of thy tabrets and of thy pipes was prepared in thee in the day thou wast created. Thou art the anointed cherub that covereth and I have set thee so; thou wast upon the holy mountain of God; thou hast walked up and down in the midst of the stones of fire. Thou wast perfect in thy ways from the day that thou wast created, till iniquity was found in thee . . . Thine heart was lifted up because of thy beauty, thou hast

corrupted thy wisdom by reason of thy brightness: I
will cast thee to the ground, I will lay thee before
kings, that they may behold thee. KJV.

Once more, the reason some biblical authorities interpret
this passage of Ezekiel as referring to an evil, fallen, angelic
being is that they take the metaphors literally. Let's look at
these metaphors and decipher them according to Semitic
figures of speech.

By reading the above passage of Ezekiel, one can understand the reason that Bible interpreters miscontrued the
prophet's metaphorical phrases. If one should accept the
above metaphors literally, one may ask, is Ezekiel writing
about a human being? After all, one reasons that the king of
Tyre was never in Eden and he was never an anointed
cherub. This is exactly how some interpreters reasoned
when they concluded that Ezekiel was writing about a
supernatural being.

But we must keep in mind that Ezekiel has been instructed by a spiritual revelation, "To take up a lamentation over the king of Tyre," and not over a fallen angel. The
prophet uses vivid, dramatic terminology typical of Near
Eastern speakers and writers.

"You were the seal of wisdom, and the crown of beauty,"
(Aramaic text) means that the king and the city of Tyre had
complete, unsurpassed wisdom, for it was a city of perfection. The people of Tyre were builders of magnificent pal-
aces, temples, shrines, and other edifices, and were makers
of articles of great beauty, which many other cities were
unable to manufacture. Tyre was never surpassed until
modern times for its naval power and for its works of brass,
ivory, gold and silver. Even today, the fine brass of Lebanon
is world famous and is exported to many countries.

"Thou wast in Eden." In this metaphor, Tyre is likened
to the earthly paradise of Eden, the garden of God. The land
was abundant with water and fertile fields. "The precious

stones" refer to the amassed wealth of that ancient city. "The anointed cherub" means the king of Tyre protected the city. In this passage, the expression to be "upon the holy mountain of God," refers to Mount Lebanon because of its great beauty. To be "perfect in thy ways" signifies the city and the king who did not do anything wrong; they did not covet or invade other lands or countries, and they were content with their own wisdom and trade with other nations.

Remember, this prophecy is a lamentation. The king of Tyre and the city were doomed. They trusted in their own strength and wisdom but the people and the city were destroyed.

And now we come to the third major passage of scripture found in the book of Revelaton:

> And there was war in heaven: Michael and his angels fought against the dragon; and the dragon fought and his angels, And prevailed not; neither was their place found any more in heaven. And the great dragon was cast out, that old serpent, called the Devil, and Satan, which deceiveth the whole world; he was cast out into the earth, and his angels were cast out with him . . . Therefore rejoice ye heavens, and ye that dwell in them. Woe to the inhabitants of the earth and of the sea! for the devil is come down unto you, having great wrath because he knoweth that he hath but a short time. Rev. 12:7–12, KJV.

The word *Revelation* in Aramaic is *GILYANA*. The root of the word is *GALA* and means "to reveal," "to uncover," "to predict," and "to foretell." The book of Revelation is a series of dreams or visions that deals with worldwide issues on both an exoteric and an esoteric level. It involves the continuing unveiling of the Christ in Jesus, in the individual, in the Church, the State and the universe. It contains over one thousand symbols. The symbols point to an idea, a truth or an event. According to historical records the book of Revelation was at first rejected, and then around 395 A.D. it was accepted. The final canon was selected at the Council of Carthage.

The point to bear in mind is that the book with its symbols must not be taken literally. There was never a war in heaven, nor was there a rebellion that God couldn't take care of. There are many different interpretations, both historically and metaphysically, of the verses in Revelation, Chapter 12. The dragon symbolizes earthly power, opposition and enmity. Pagan rulers from the very beginning were aware of the growth of the Christian movement and its influence on their people. The dragon also represents false ideas that one may hold in consciousness. Michael and his angels and the war in heaven symbolize the struggle between truth and error. The word "angel" in Aramaic means God's thought or counsel. In other words, the dragon, the gross deception, the opposition to the truth, is totally defeated.

FALLEN ANGELS

The last and final area of the Bible that supposedly deals with the origin of Lucifer and his fallen angels is found in 2 Peter 2:4, which says, "For God spared not the angels that sinned but cast them down to hell, and delivered them into chains of darkness, to be reserved unto judgment." KJV. Before pursuing Peter's statement further, we need to understand the use of the term "angel" in the Bible.

Once again, we are facing Eastern imagery and use of metaphors, for the term "angels" in Aramaic has many meanings. It can signify "ministers," "messengers," "holy men," "pious men," "good people," "sons of God," and "God's counsel and thoughts."

In Psalm 104:4, the writer states that God, "maketh his angels spirits; and his ministers a flaming fire." Thus angels are "spirit," subject neither to sin nor to physical laws. Spirit is intangible and indestructible; therefore no heavenly angels could have "sinned."

Now let us return to Peter's statement as quoted above. The apostle alludes to the incident related in Genesis 6:1–5:

> And it came to pass, when men began to multiply on the face of the earth, and daughters were born unto them, that the sons of God saw the daughters of men that they were fair; and they took them wives of all which they chose. And the Lord said, *My spirit shall not always strive with man* (Idiom: I have become impatient) for that he also is flesh; yet his days shall be an hundred and twenty years. KJV.

The term "sons of God" here refers to the descendants of Seth, who were good, pious men. But these men of God had decided to break from the lineage of Seth and intermarry with the descendants of Cain. These pious men turned from God and began to worship idols, adopt pagan beliefs, and indulge in immoral acts which brought suffering and grave illness.

The Semitic metaphors used by Peter are to be understood thus: "Cast them down into hell" means they would suffer for their evil deeds and practices. "For God spared not the angels that sinned" means these pious "fallen" men were not to be spared the consequences of their own misdirected behavior. "Delivered them into chains of darkness" indicates they became enslaved to sin—that is, to their erroneous ways. Ignorance would hold them in their error and evil actions.

Such figurative expressions are well understood in Eastern languages, but we in the West have taken them literally and have founded unwarranted doctrines of "fallen angels and demons."

POETICAL PHILOSOPHY

The book of Job was written to answer a philosophical question, "Why do good people suffer?" It is written in a poetical philosophical style. The book is difficult to understand, because not only were many verses not clearly translated, but the book is filled with idioms and metaphors. The book of Job is a drama, and again it must not be taken literally.

The author of Job portrays God as an oriental potentate. Perhaps you have read the book. "Anna and the King of Siam" or have seen the Rodgers and Hammerstein musical, "The King and I." In the musical Rodgers and Hammerstein portray all the children of the king marching before him on an appointed day. Oriental kings have so many children that they do not have time to see them one at a time, so they have an appointed day where all the sons of the king come together to meet with their father. There is only one son he will see apart from all of his other sons, and that is the crown prince. The Eastern writer of the book of Job portrays God as an oriental king receiving his children on an appointed day: "Now there was a day when the sons of God came to present themselves before the Lord." But the author goes on to say that, "Satan came also among them," and the Lord God, instead of carrying on a conversation with his sons, struck up a conversation with Satan. (Satan here represents an accuser—evil advisor.)

The Lord asked Satan if he had considered his servant Job since there has been no one like him. He reveres the Lord God and turns from evil completely. But according to the story, Satan suggested that Job only served and revered God and rejected evil because God had protected him, blessed his house and his children and everything that he owned. God had blessed the works of Job's hands and everything he possessed had increased. But, if all that were to change, the Lord God would soon see how much Job would be faithful to Him. God then gave Satan permission to test Job severely, but he could not touch his life.

Then in the second chapter of Job the sons of God came to present themselves once again, and Satan was with them. The Lord was indeed greatly impressed with Job's faithfulness even though he had lost everything. Robbers had raided the oxen and the asses and had slain many of Job's servants with the edge of the sword; lightning had struck from heaven and burned up the sheep and the shepherds; the Chaldeans had invaded the land, stolen the camels, and also had more of Job's servants slain by the edge of the sword. Job's sons and daughters were eating and drinking in their oldest brother's home and there came a strong wind from the desert, and the house collapsed killing all of his sons and daughters.

When Job heard all of this terribly tragic news, his reply was, "Naked I came out of my mother's womb, and naked shall I return; the Lord gave, and the Lord has taken away; blessed be the name of the Lord." In all these catastrophes Job did not sin nor did he blaspheme against the Lord. The Lord was very proud of Job and quickly informed Satan, "Have you considered my servant Job, that there is none like him in the earth, an innocent and upright man, one who reveres God, and turns away from evil? He still holds fast to his integrity, *although you provoked me against him*, to destroy him without cause." There is some subtle humor in what the Lord God says to Satan, ". . . although you provoked me against him." The Lord God in essence says, "The devil made me do it." This entire episode with God and Satan never happened. Again, we must keep in mind that this is a drama.

Once again Satan is not impressed and suggests that he should touch Job in some way, "Skin for skin, yea, all that a man has will he give for his life, to save it. But put forth thy hand now, and touch his flesh or his bone, and he will curse thee to thy face." The Lord God was again provoked by Satan's suggestion and allowed this evil emissary to touch the physical body of Job, and then, the poor man was struck with skin cancer. While Job was suffering so very badly, his wife even taunted him, and with great disdain accusingly spoke, "Do you still hold fast your integrity? Curse God, and die." Job was not moved by his wife's accusations and taunts, but he replied to her, "You speak as one of the foolish women speaks. We have indeed received God's blessings, now shall we not also receive his afflictions?" In all these great misfortunes Job did not sin nor did he blaspheme against God with his lips.

Now the writer of the book of Job begins to develop the philosophical arguments: Job has four friends who come and sit around him while he laments in the ash heap. Job must now argue his way out of his situation with his friends who accuse him of cheating others and therefore he is reaping what he has sown. His friends represent the philosophical and religious beliefs of Job's time. In the very end of the story, everything is restored to Job because he comes to a great realization which answers the philosophical question —"Why do good people suffer?"

Job reached the conclusion that no one was one hundred percent good and perfect. Therefore, we bring our disasters upon ourselves, but the grace of God restores us even in the midst of our tribulations and afflictions. Job learned humility and he learned not to trust in his own integrity.

Then Job answered the Lord, and said, I know that thou canst do all these things, and that no purpose can be hid from thee. Who am I to think that I can give counsel without knowledge? Therefore thou hast declared to me that I have uttered that which I did not understand, things too wonderful for me which I did not know. Hear me, I pray thee, and I will speak; I will ask thee, and declare thou to me; I have heard of thee by the hearing of the ear, but now my eye sees thee. Therefore, I will keep silent, and repent in dust and ashes. Job 42:1–6, Lamsa translation.

The lesson was learned. Job was restored and had greater wealth than before. (See Job 42:10–17).

CHAPTER 7

The Seventh Key
Amplification

The final key is Near Eastern amplification. Sometimes this key can be very difficult for Western readers of the Bible to understand. I chose the word, "amplification" over the word "exaggeration" simply because our culture and way of thinking does not accept exaggeration, especially in a "sacred book."

In the Near Eastern culture, to amplify an event and to picturesquely color a situation is totally acceptable and agreeable to Eastern listeners. The Bible is filled with many passages of amplification. The biblical writers amplify in order to glorify an event. An illustration one might find useful is: Eastern amplification is like a painting on canvas. When one frames the painting it begins to stand out. The frame helps "amplify" the picture. Thus, many episodes in the scriptures are "framed," that is, amplified.

Dr. Rihbany gives us some insight into this particular Eastern characteristic.

A Syrian's chief purpose in a conversation is to convey an impression by whatever suitable means, and not to deliver his message in scientifically accurate terms. He expects to be judged not by what he

115

says, but by what he means. . . . It is also because
the Syrian loves to speak in pictures, and to subordinate literal accuracy to the total impression of an
utterance, that he makes such extensive use of figurative language. . . . Just as the Oriental (Easterner)
loves to flavor his food strongly and to dress in
bright colors, so is he fond of metaphor, exaggeration, and positiveness in speech. To him mild accuracy is weakness.[1]

When I first began to work with Dr. George Lamsa in
1965, I did not know about this Eastern characteristic.
After working with him for awhile, I finally learned not to
take what he said at face value. Dr. Lamsa enjoyed making
an impression by increasing the numbers, which was also
typical of Eastern writers of the Bible. At different times
when I desired to know the exact situation with accuracy
and detail I would use the Aramaic expression, "Amen,
amen," or "Truly, truly," which means "Tell it to me this
time without amplification."

Jesus throughout his teachings often used the expression,
"Amen, amen I say unto you," or "Verily, verily I say to
you." This Eastern style of speech means "Do not cut in
half what I am saying to you; there is no amplification," or
"It is straight from the shoulder." Eastern people expected
their speakers to amplify. Hence, when the phrase "Amen,
amen" is spoken the listeners know to take seriously exactly what was said.

CONTRADICTIONS IN SCRIPTURAL TEXTS

The seemingly apparent contradictions we find in the
Scriptures are due to amplification, especially in regard to
numbers and different locations. As stated earlier, Eastern
people do not care for exactness or literal accuracy. To
them it makes no difference whether there were 500 or 200

present, or, for that matter, even a thousand. This is why we have several varying accounts of Jesus multiplying the loaves and fish. One gospel writer said he fed 5,000. Another writer said he fed 4,000. Again, it depends on the writer. He flavors the event the way he chooses. What we must realize is that Jesus fed hungry men, women, and children. The need was met. We need not be concerned as to exactly how many were present to be fed.

THE STORY OF THE RESURRECTION

The resurrecton of Jesus Christ has been "under fire" by many theologians because of the seemingly, contradictory accounts found in the four gospels of Matthew, Mark, Luke and John. But again the object of the Eastern writers was to tell one and the same story, that the Christ came forth victoriously from the tomb. The event to them occurred, but now the framework around the event depended on each individual writer. This kind of reasoning puts serious doubts in the minds of Western Bible readers. But an Easterner isn't the slightest bit disturbed by the amplified numbers, contradictory events or change of localities recorded by the writers of the four gospels. Dr. George Lamsa believed in the resurrection of Jesus Christ. He used to say, "Any time eleven Eastern men like the apostles would agree on any one subject it would have to be true."

Eastern speakers also enjoy expressing their ideas in blanket statements and sweeping utterances. You will find such expressions in the Bible as "And at even' when the sun did set, they brought unto him *all that were diseased,* and them that were possessed of devils, and *all the city* was gathered together at the door." Mark 1:32-33, KJV.

In the book of Genesis we find a very fascinating and "all encompassing" statement made to a beloved daughter. Abraham has sent his servant to Haran to obtain a wife for his son Isaac. Eleazar, the servant, arrived in Haran and went among the Arameans, and there he met Rebekah at the well. Rebekah and her family were kin to Abraham. (For the detailed story read Genesis, Chapter 24.) After Eleazar had completed his transaction and Rebekah was departing her family, her brother Laban and her mother pronounced a great blessing upon Rebekah. "And they blessed Rebekah, their sister, and said to her, You are our sister, *be the mother of thousands and of millions*, and let your descendants inherit the lands of their enemies." Gen. 24: 60. Can you imagine being the mother of thousands and millions?

Also throughout the Old Testament we find other amplifications. Samson killed "*a thousand soldiers* with the jawbone of an ass," "the stars of heaven fought from their orbits. They fought from heaven against Caesara, the enemy of Israel." Abraham's descendants were to be as "the sand of the seashore and the stars of the universe." The Lord brought quail from the sea and they fell exhausted to the earth "three feet high." The walls of the cities of Canaan were considered great and "fenced up to heaven." There are many more passages like these that I have mentioned.

As one begins to understand the Eastern style of writing, it will become easier to detect such statements. Remember, none of these expressions were written to deceive the reader or listener but to glorify the event and to make an impression.

Descriptive Poetry

The poetical amplification is very beautiful in the Scriptures. When people were in deep mourning it was said, "The sun refused to shine, and the moon and the stars no longer gave their light." When there is great happiness and joy among the people it is stylized in the following manner, "The mountains danced and the hills leaped and skipped, and the trees clapped their hands." When they wished to express the idea of solemnity when Moses received the ten commandments, "The mountains shook, the earth trembled, darkness, lightning, thunder, and noises were heard from Mount Sinai."

We must also keep in mind that not all recorded events in the Scriptures are amplified nor is everything metaphor. One has to understand what he is reading. By now the reader of the seven keys no doubt has a clearer idea of what it is to see the Scriptures through Eastern eyes.

PART TWO

The Commentary

Chapters 8, 9

CHAPTER 8

The Seven Keys
And the Old Testament

In this chapter and in the one that follows we will be applying the seven keys to various passages of Scripture chosen at random from the Old Testament. In some of the biblical verses we will use only one or two of the keys, and in some other passages we may have to use more.

THE NAMES OF GOD

Our English word "God" is derived from the German language and means "the good," but in the Near Eastern languages—Aramaic, Hebrew, and Arabic—the term "God" has a deeper significance than simply "the good."

The Aramaic *ALAHA*, the Hebrew *ELOHIM*, and the Arabic *ALLAH* all come from Aramaic and Hebrew root words *AIL* and *EL*, and mean "to aid," "to help," "to defend," "to sustain," and "to succor." The name of God in the biblical languages also has various subordinate applications which express the idea of might, power and strength. Thus, God is thought of as All Might, All Power and All Strength. And in the East in general God is understood as the very essence of all life and as the great Provider.

The names of God found in the Hebrew Scriptures came by revelation. The patriarchs and prophets had mystical encounters with the Presence we call God. It was from these men of vision and from their personal, subjective realizations, that the different names of God were revealed and recorded. (According to the Koran, God has ninety-nine excellent names.) Once again, dreams and visions were the means by which the various names of God became known.

Of all the names of God, the one that usually holds the greatest interest and fascination for most readers of the Bible is the name that was revealed to Moses on Mount Sinai, which has been translated as the "I AM." "And God said unto Moses, I AM THAT I AM: And he said, thus shall you say to the children of Israel, I AM hath sent me to you." Exodus 3:14, KJV. The Aramaic text reads, "And Alaha said to Moses, *AHIYAH ASHARA HIYAH*. And he said, thus shall you say to the sons of Israel, *AHIYAH* has sent me to you." The Hebrew and Aramaic texts in their original forms are identical.

Most Bible translators admit that it is very difficult to translate the term *AHIYAH*. In English we refer to this name as Jehovah. Most biblical scholars believe the name comes from the verb *HAYAH*—"to be." Dr. Lamsa suggests the word be translated as "The Living One."[1] The Semitic term implies something which exists in and of itself, an Essence which was, is and is to come. In other words, *AHIYAH* simply IS and is ever constant. God-realization is truly transmental and transphenomenal, and is therefore indescribable.

Another name for God used in the Near East is the word *ITHEA*. This word signifies "it" or "essence," the very origin of a thing. Interestingly, in Western Aramaic, the term *ITHEA* became *ITHEO*, and later on the Greeks used the same word, changing it to *THEOS* or *THEO*. To refer to God, then, as the "It" is in accordance with Semitic thought because God as "It" means "the very essence and substance of life." In English we simply translate all the varying

Semitic terms such as *ALAHA, AHIYAH, ITHEA* and many other names in one way—God.

Although I have presented a somewhat academic explanation of the various names of God, to an Easterner the whole matter goes deeper still. When a Semite refers to God, he prefers that you *feel* rather than just intellectualize his meaning. In other words, God may be referred to intellectually, but an understanding of God is only realized intuitively and from the heart of man. It is impossible for a Semite to try to press the meaning of God, who is life itself, into a uniform dogma or into a rigid mold for the logical Western mind.

The men in the Bible knew Alaha as a living presence, and from their subjectively charged experience, certain names of God came into usage or existence. As an example: "And it came to pass when Abram was ninety-nine years old, the Lord came in a revelation to Abram and said to him, I am the almighty Alaha (God)." Gen. 17:1, Aramaic text. The Hebrew term *AILSHADDAY*, translated here as "almighty," also means "self-sufficient," "sustainer," "nourisher," "omnipotent," and "sovereign." In addition, the name "almighty" implies a power which was in vivid contrast to the helplessness of the pagan idols, which were completely incapable of sustaining their worshippers.

And so, when Alaha communed with Abraham, revealing Himself as the true Nourisher and Sustainer of life, Abraham grew in his realization of God and was strengthened internally and renewed in his spirit. The Hebrew patriarchs came to many realizations through the spiritual infilling and all encompassing Presence of the Living God.

GOD IS ONE

And God said, let us make man in our image, after our likeness: and let them have dominion over the fish of the sea, and over the fowl of the air, and over the cattle, and over all the earth, and over every creeping thing that creepth upon the earth. Gen. 1:26, KJV.

To whom was God addressing the "us" and the "our?" The Hebrew writers of the Bible tell us that God is one, and this belief in the oneness of God has preserved Judaism and unified the Jewish people against much opposition and persecution over the centuries. "Hear, O Israel, the Lord our God is One." Deut. 6:4.

Some Jewish commentators suggest that the writer refers to God's majesty and power and therefore these words should be interpreted as denoting "the plurality of power." Then again, there are Christian commentators who believe this implies the doctrine of the Trinity. Certain other theologians believe that God addressed the angels.

In Eastern countries, however, kings, bishops, princes, high-ranking governmental authorities and ecclesiastical officials—in accordance with standard usage in Semitic languages—use the plural form when speaking of themselves. This plural form, which is the same one used in the Bible, is called the "plural of respect." It is never used by the common people.

The "plural of respect" has been misunderstood by many Western interpreters of the Bible who are unfamiliar with Semitic culture and mannerisms of speech. Some have concluded that there are three persons in the Godhead, though such a concept of the plurality of God was alien and repulsive to the Hebrew people and they fought bitterly against it. In fact, the doctrine of the Trinity was not introduced until 325 A.D. at the Nicean Council. Before that time both Jews and Christians believed and worshipped the one God only; neither the prophets, Jesus, nor his apostles had ever hinted that there was more than one God, though apparently it must have been difficult for the Western world to comprehend the Semitic idea of one God. The ancient Aramaïc-speaking Church of the East, however, still maintains that there is only one God revealed in three *KENOMAYE,* i.e., attributes of manifestations. These three *KENOMAYE* are known as Mind, Wisdom and Life (Consciousness).

CHERUBIM

So he drove out the man; and he placed at the east of the garden of Eden Cherubims, and a flaming sword which turned every way, to keep the way of the tree of life. Gen. 3:24, KJV.

The Hebrew word *K'ROBIM* and Aramaic word *K'RO-BEY,* cherubim, mean guardian angels. According to the ancient Semitic belief, angels were messengers, but the chief function of the cherubim was to guard and protect. Hence, cherubim were guardian angels. The images of cherubim were placed on the thrones of kings as a symbol of protection. Moses made images of the cherubim and placed them over the ark of the covenant to protect it from thieves. The cherubim were fashioned by Moses upon the top of the ark to form what was called "the Mercy Seat." The Presence of God would commune with Moses from the "Mercy Seat" above the ark which was present in the tabernacle. (See Ex. 25:17–22).

In biblical days it was customary for a king to place men servants with swords at the entrance of his sacred garden to keep people away. Thus, the symbology of the East is carried out in the story of Adam and Eve. In this instance the cherubim and flaming sword are symbolic of God's counsel guarding the progeny of man (the tree of life) from further immorality. Thus, the moral law is inherent in all races.

All nations and peoples who surrender completely to immorality perish in one manner or another. The people of Sodom and Gomorrah, the worshippers of Baal, and the descendants of the early inhabitants of Palestine had all perished because of immorality. They all destroyed themselves with riotous and degenerative living. In such instances the biological life force becomes weak and so diseased that it cannot replicate healthy physical beings.

The cherubim, the moral law, is a part of man and operates instinctively. The moral law is known to all and therefore guides, protects and guards man.

THE MARK OF CAIN

> And the Lord said unto him, Therefore whosoever slayeth Cain, vengeance shall be taken on him sevenfold. And the Lord set a mark upon Cain, lest any finding him should kill him. Gen. 4:15, KJV.

Until recent days assassins in Semitic lands were branded as one would brand cattle. The mark bore witness that the criminal had been punished for his crime. Even today in many Moslem countries robbers and criminals are punished by cutting off their noses, legs, hands or arms. According to the biblical episode, Cain knew he was to leave the beautiful land of Eden. He was to become a wanderer. Since Cain was doomed to be a vagabond, he wanted protection. In the East when a man flees his country and takes refuge among a foreign people and land, everyone wants to know why. Any individual who leaves his kinsmen, traditions and religion is looked upon as an outlaw and is unwelcome. Cain wanted assurance from God that he would not be put to death by strangers.

Cain was exiled from the land of Eden, and the mark was the evidence and sign that he had been punished. God assured Cain that anyone who would slay him would be punished sevenfold. The number "seven," as I have already mentioned, is frequently used in the Bible and considered a holy number. It is symbolic of the seven planets known to the ancient world. The Bible writer depicted the Lord God using the number "seven" because Eastern people used that number extensively and could relate to its significance in the story of Cain.

BIRTH CONTROL

> And Judah said unto Onan, Go in unto thy brother's wife, and marry her, and raise up seed to thy brother. And Onan knew that the seed should not be his; and it came to pass, when he went into his brother's wife, that he spilled it on the ground, lest he should give seed to his brother. And the thing which he did displeased the Lord: wherefore he slew him also. Gen. 38:8–10, KJV.

From the very beginning, Semitic people believed that the continuity of life was in posterity. They also believed that when a man died without a son he was deprived of his immortality. Therefore, in an Eastern family when one of the married brothers died without an heir, custom dictated that another brother must marry his widowed sister-in-law and raise an heir for the deceased.

Onan was unwilling to raise an heir for his brother who had died. He knew the heir would eventually become a rival to him as generally happens in the East. This is the reason Onan practiced this form of birth control.

Today we know that the continuance of life is not in one's descendants but in the survival of the race. Thousands of men had sacrificed their lives for the faith of their people and country and had left no heirs. Martyrs and saints also had surrendered to death so that others might live. Certainly these individuals are not cut off from the "tree of life" because they left no descendants or heirs. We realize that not all branches in a tree produce fruit, but all the branches share in the nourishing of the fruits. So it is with the human family.

But in the ancient biblical days everything was attributed to God. Therefore, it was believed that the Lord God slew Onan. Typically, Onan's death was interpreted by Easterners as God's displeasure and punishment for his refusal to raise an heir for his brother.

AND GOD REMEMBERED

And God heard their groaning, and God remembered his covenant with Abraham, with Isaac, and with Jacob. And God looked upon the children of Israel, and God had respect unto them. Ex. 2:24–25, KJV.

In the last part of verse 25, the King James Version states, "And God had respect unto them." However, the Aramaic and Hebrew texts differ from this rendering of the verse. They literally read, "And God saw the sons of Israel, and God knew." The Semitic term *YDAA* means "to know," "to notice," "to recognize," "to perceive directly," and "to apprehend immediately by the senses or by the mind." The writer tells us that God heard Israel's cries of oppression, and He remembered the agreement He had made with their forefathers. The Lord God, then, looked upon Israel and immediately apprehended the dire situation.

The expression "and God remembered," is a very significant phrase to Easterners. It strikes a deep tender response in their hearts. "The remembrance," as it is called in the Near East, is important in the daily lives of the people and in their literature. It underscores the most sensitive spirit of their poetry. Such phrases as "and I remember," "remember me," "your remembrance," and "the remembrance of those days" are just a few of the numerous similar expressions used by the Semites. Throughout the

Bible this phrase appears over and over again, "and God remembered." The phrase, however, should not be taken literally. God does not remember or forget. This is a stylized form of Eastern writing (See Gen. 8:1, 19:29 and 30:22).

It was Moses, the author of Exodus, who emphasized the fact that God had not forgotten the sons of Israel while they were in Egypt. He had been with them all the time. He had raised Joseph to a high position, second only to that of a king. God had increased their numbers abundantly, blessed their flocks, and multiplied their wealth. Now it was time for Israel to be reminded of the covenant of Abraham, Isaac, and Jacob and their spiritual mission as a nation to carry the light of God.

According to the book of Genesis, God, from the beginning, had called their forefathers from Chaldea to dwell in Palestine. The covenant that God had made with the patriarchs must be fulfilled. The only way to carry out the promises was to bring the sons of Israel back to the land where their fathers had lived and were buried. The Hebrews detested city living, civil ordinances and forced labor. They were ready to return to Palestine.

God Repents

> Then came the word of the Lord unto Samuel, saying, it repenteth me that I have set up Saul to be king: for he is turned back from following me, and hath not performed my commandments. And it grieved Samuel; and he cried unto the Lord all night. 1 Sam. 15: 10–11, KJV.

Eastern writers usually describe God as a man. They often portray Him as wearing garments, having a beard, sitting in a chariot and riding in the clouds. At times they even ascribe to Him human emotions such as being sorry or happy. All these attributes are replicas of man's own characteristics. Jesus said, "God is Spirit." Spirit is intangible and noncorporeal. The Scriptures clearly state that no man has ever seen God (See John 1:18). And, because no man has ever seen God, the Eastern writers portray God in physical form giving Him human emotions.

Actually, it was Samuel who regretted having made Saul the king of Israel. Samuel sought vengeance against the Amalekites because they had harassed his people centuries ago. (See Exodus 17:8–14). According to the book of Deuteronomy, Moses had left orders that Israel should always remember what Amalek did to them when they fled Egypt and were traveling through the desert. He reminded them in detail of how Amalek met them with the sword and killed all those who were left behind when the people were faint and weary. Amalek was an enemy never to be forgotten. (See Deut. 25:17–19).

Samuel had given strict orders to Saul to slay every one of the Amalekites. Saul disobeyed those orders. As readers of the Bible, we must always keep in mind that Samuel was reared at a time when the law of the land was "an eye for an eye and a tooth for a tooth," so what was done to Israel by the Amalekites had to be repeated by Israel to the Amalekites. Such was the logic of that particular era.

God does not repent; and neither does he regret. But as was stated earlier, Eastern biblical writers often depicted God as a human being, regretting, repenting, and even changing His mind.

PAYING HOMAGE TO A PRINCE

And Jonathan gave his artillery unto his lad, and said unto him, Go, carry them to the city. And as soon as the lad was gone, David arose out of a place toward the south, and fell on his face to the ground, and bowed himself three times: and they kissed one another, and wept one with another, until David exceeded. 1 Sam. 20:40–41, KJV.

According to the Eastern custom, government officials and noblemen bowed to the ground when greeting a royal prince or king. At times they would also kiss the shoes, knees and hand of the monarch. This custom still prevails in these Eastern lands which continue the ancient practices and are governed by kings. In those days kings and princes were looked upon as deities and were often worshipped by the people. When David saw Jonathan, he fell with his face to the ground and made obeisance. After all, Jonathan was the crown prince and heir to the throne of Israel.

Kissing among Eastern men was a common custom, a custom that is still fondly cherished and respectfully practiced. For instance, Eastern men who are friends and of the same social status usually kiss one another on both cheeks and sometimes quite noisily.

David was Jonathan's brother-in-law. They knew that they would not see each other again and therefore wept and kissed in the typical Eastern fashion. In fact, the Aramaic text says that David wept more than Jonathan.

A WILLINGNESS TO LOSE ONE'S OWN LIFE

I am distressed for thee, my brother Jonathan: very pleasant hast thou been unto me: thy love to me was wonderful, passing the love of women. 2 Sam. 1:26, KJV.

David, mourning over Jonathan, his brother-in-law, poured out his soul in song. Jonathan had saved David's life from his father, King Saul. His love for David was so great that he had risked the anger of his father, and possibly the punishment of exile or death. Saul was very bitter towards his son because he knew that Jonathan had been helping David. The king had rebuked his son on many occasions.

In Aramaic, the word "love" is used only in a spiritual manner and in no way refers to sexual relationship. It is used in the Scriptures to refer to loving your enemies, loving your country and ruler, and loving God. In the Near East men address one another as "my beloved." The apostle Paul uses these terms in his epistles. Jesus also said, "A new commandment I give you, that you love one another; just as I have loved you, that you also love one another." John 13:34. Pure love is the cohesive force that binds humanity together.

The phrase, ". . . your love to me was wonderful, passing the love of women," means that Jonathan's love was incomparable. David refers to spiritual love. Jonathan was willing to die for the sake of his brother-in-law. Jesus said, "There is no greater love than this, that a man lay down his life for the sake of his friends." John 15:13.

THE BEARD AND DISGRACE

> Wherefore Hanun took David's servants, and shaved off the one-half of their beards, and cut off their garments in the middle, even to their buttocks, and sent them away. 2 Sam. 10:4, KJV.

It is very difficult to convey to Western people how Easterners feel about their beards. It was a very ancient sacred belief of the Hebrews that a man's strength was in his hair and that it contained life. Samson believed that his strength was in his hair, because it served as a reminder of the divine promises which God had revealed to his mother and father. Samson was bound by the Nazarite vow. No razor was to touch his head. In the Near East, if anyone should make an unkind or unwise remark about another man's mustache or beard, or even dare to curse the beard of another man's father, that man would be in deep trouble. He could lose his life over such remarks.

Eastern men love to swear on their beards. There is a great deal of body language with the beard also. For instance, if an Easterner strokes his beard while you are speaking, this means he does not believe what you are saying. If an Easterner holds his beard while you speak or teach, that means he trusts in what you say.

When a nobleman is disgraced or a priest is defrocked, half of his beard is shaved. When women are punished for acts of immorality, their hair is shaved and their garments are torn as a sign of mourning over the deed they have done. All those who look upon them know they have been punished (See 1 Cor. 11:5). The beard is looked upon so highly that at times people will swear by the beards of a prophet, saint, or king. Some Moslems believe that a few hairs from the beard of their holy prophet Mohammed were preserved. Such holy relics are priceless. Pilgrims come from all over the world to visit holy places containing such relics.

The king of Ammon was suspicious of David's sympathies for the passing of the king's father. It was not uncommon for enemies of a certain kingdom to take advantage of such an opportunity in order to spy within the city. When mourning a king, princes and noblemen are engaged in lamenting the deceased; therefore the spies who are pretending to mourn are generally free to roam through the city and study its fortifications, its entrances and exits. Such defenses are kept very secret. Also sources of water and wells were generally kept hidden so that the city's water supply would not be cut off during a siege. If the wells and other water sources were disconnected, the city would be forced to surrender.

David wanted to avenge his honor when he heard that his ambassadors had been disgraced by the king of Ammon. He commanded his men to stay at Jericho until their beards grew out once again. In Eastern countries a man's beard is a symbol of his dignity, honor, virility and maturity. If the ambassadors had returned to Jerusalem with half-shaven beards, they would have become a laughingstock.

THE LORD STRUCK THE CHILD

And Nathan departed unto his house. And the Lord struck the child that Uriah's wife bare unto David, and it was very sick. 2 Sam. 12:15, KJV.

In biblical days health, death, misfortunes and sicknesses were looked upon as acts of God. When people did something wrong and misfortune would come to them, it was believed that God had brought the calamity as punishment. Then again when others prospered, it was believed that God had brought wealth. They believed that nothing happened without God's knowledge and approval.

In those days, when religion was in its infancy and the knowledge of God was limited to a few people, men did not realize that most of the things which happened to them were manifestations of their own actions.

God does not discriminate among his children. It is man who attributes discrimination to God. For instance, the Bible says that God struck the first child of David and Bathsheba with sickness and then loved their second child, even giving him a nickname. (See 2 Sam. 12:24–25). This was the belief of the people in those days. Jesus taught that God is love and we know "love" does not author sickness or disease.

POLYGAMY

But King Solomon loved many strange women, together with the daughter of Pharaoh, women of the

Moabites, Ammonites, Edomites, Zidonians, and Hittites; Of the nations concerning which the Lord said unto the children of Israel, Ye shall not go in to them, neither shall they come in unto you: for surely they will turn away your heart after their gods: Solomon clave unto these in love. And he had seven-hundred wives, princesses, and three hundred concubines: and his wives turned away his heart. 1 Kings 11:1–3, KJV.

From time immemorial, polygamy has been prevalent in the Near East, the Middle East, and many other countries. Constant wars caused an imbalance between the male and female populations. Men practiced polygamy, not only to replenish the population, but also for economic and political reasons. In those days alliances were made through marriages. Therefore, Solomon married seven hundred women, forming alliances with kings, princes and other powerful leaders.

Another example is the king of Tyre who made an alliance with King Ahab by giving him his daughter, Jezebel, in marriage. Pharaoh also made alliances with King Solomon. Marriage sealed the agreement. King Solomon became the son-in-law of all the rulers with whom he made treaties. This was the reason there was peace during his reign.

Nevertheless, Solomon's marriages with foreign women were contrary to the laws of Moses. These wives of Solomon stole his heart and led him to worship pagan gods and thus contributed to the downfall of his kingdom.

Solomon had acquired considerable wisdom and experience in settling quarrels between his wives. This was evidenced by his clever judgment when two women sought justice from his hands. (See 1 Kings 3:16–28).

THE MANTLE

> So he departed thence, and found Elisha the son of
> Shaphat, who was plowing with twelve yoke of oxen
> before him, and he with the twelfth: and Elijah
> passed by him, and cast his mantle upon him. And
> he left the oxen, and ran after Elijah, and said, Let
> me, I pray thee, kiss my father and my mother, and
> then I will follow thee. And he said unto him, Go
> back again: for what have I done to thee? And he
> returned back from him, and took a yoke of oxen,
> and slew them, and boiled their flesh with the in-
> struments of the oxen, and gave unto the people,
> and they did eat. Then he arose, and went after Eli-
> jah, and ministered unto him. 1 Kings 19:19–21,
> KJV.

Evidently Elijah was growing old and needed a successor.
His battles with the prophets of Baal and with the king and
queen of Israel had sapped his strength. Furthermore, the
cunning queen, Jezebel, continually sought to take his life.

When the prophet was returning home from Mount Ho-
reb, he passed through a large field where there were twelve
plows. Elisha was one of the plowers. The moment Elijah
saw Elisha the Spirit of the Lord, that is, an inner voice told
him that Elisha was his successor. Then he suddenly took
off his mantle and threw it over Elisha. This act signified
that Elisha was to inherit the prophetic office of Elijah and
that the battles of Elijah were to become the battles of
Elisha. The people feared and respected the prophets more
than they did their kings. Elisha was overjoyed at the pros-
pect of becoming a prophet. He accepted his call by immediately sacrificing the oxen, boiling the meat, and giving
it to the people as a thank offering.

The prophet Elijah was surprised by Elisha's ready accep-
tance of the prophetic office. For a few moments Elijah
thought that Elisha might change his mind, so he tested

him out and said to him, "Go back again; for what have I done to you?" But Elisha had shown his determination by following the prophet. He served Elijah faithfully and studied with him until the day he wore the mantle of his master permanently.

POETICAL METAPHORS

For ye shall go out with joy, and be led forth with peace: the mountains and the hills shall break forth before you into singing, and all the trees of the field shall clap their hands. Instead of the thorn shall come up the fir tree, and instead of the brier shall come up the myrtle tree: and it shall be to the Lord for a name, for an everlasting sign that shall not be cut off. Isaiah 55:12–13, KJV.

Isaiah refers to the Remnant of Israel. The Remnant was to return peacefully to their homeland and not as their fore-fathers who had left Egypt in the midst of fear. The Gentile nations among whom the Remnant of Israel was dwelling would offer them help, and according to Isaiah, nature also was to share in Israel's glorious return. The trees were to be glad and clap their hands, that is, Israel was to receive praise.

"Instead of the thorn shall come up the fir tree" means that instead of difficulties, Israel will have blessings and harmony. "Instead of the brier shall come up the myrtle tree" signifies that Israel will no longer be harassed but will have joy and open reception. The Gentiles will praise God's name for his faithfulness in returning the Jews.

The prophet uses poetical figurative speech. Eastern people understand this clearly and do not take it literally. They know that trees and fields clapping their hands and the hills and mountains singing means that nature shares in man's happiness and sorrow.

CONCLUSION

As one can readily see, the Bible is more clearly understood when one is familiar with the seven keys that help unlock the Scriptures. The preceding commentaries are only a few passages of the Old Testament. There is much more to know and understand. But now we are ready to begin our look at the New Testament in the light of the seven keys.

CHAPTER 9

The Seven Keys
And the New Testament

HEAVEN

Where and what is heaven? Is heaven a place for life here-after? Once again we turn to the Aramaic language for meaning. The Aramaic word for heaven is *SHMAYA*. This compound noun derives its meaning from *SHEM*, "name," and *YAH*, "God." Thus, the root meaning of the word, "heaven" is "the name of God." The ancients considered the heavens to be the habitation of God, as well as a decla-ration of His glory and wondrous works. The Biblical psalmist puts it this way, "The heavens sing the songs of God; and the firmament reveals the works of His hand." Psalm 19:1, Aramaic text.

That this Aramaic word which means "heaven" also means "sky," "cosmos," or "universe," is consistent with the belief in ancient biblical days that God lived in high places, far away from humanity. Pagan temples and shrines were built on high hills and mountains because people be-lieved contact with the gods was made more easily in high places than in the lowlands. (Some biblical writers believed that the clouds were God's chariots.) But many of the He-brew prophets, and Jesus, understood that God is everywhere. Jesus instructed us, "When you pray, pray in this manner, Our Father who is in heaven." Heaven means "the universe" or "everywhere." Jesus also said that God is Spirit, that is, everywhere. (See John 4:24).

When Paul stood before the men of Athens in the court at Aeropagus, he declared the universal Presence of God as he said, "For the God who made the world and all things therein, and who is the Lord of heaven and earth, does not dwell in temples made with hands; . . . *For in Him we live and move and have our being*, as some of your own wise men have said, for we are his kindred." Acts 17:24–28, Aramaic text. This realization is truly the key to understanding the meaning of "heaven."

The term "heaven" was also used metaphorically in the Bible to express the idea of peace, order and harmony. The ancient savants in studying the heavens observed the order and harmony of the stars and planets. So the prophets, through their teachings, endeavored to show mankind that they also could function as the heavenly bodies, that is, harmoniously and in an orderly manner. When living in times of peace, prosperity and tranquility, Easterners often say, "We are in heaven." Figuratively, "heaven" also means a greater consciousness, i.e., one in which thoughts of lack and fear disappear. Thus one can readily see that the term "heaven" also depicts a state of being and not just a specified location.

Geographically speaking, we are in heaven now. The planet we call earth is present in a vast cosmos. Actually, there isn't a man anywhere who can honestly tell the human family exactly where it is. The earth, being somewhere in a tremendous universe of galaxies, has no starting point from which to measure. Man has many theories, but he does not know with any certainty how the universe began, or how—or if—it will end. All he knows is that we are somewhere in space.

Jesus often referred to the "kingdom of heaven" in his talks. The kingdom of heaven which he preached and expounded by means of parables was to be a universal state ruled by him, through his teachings and commandments. This universal reign, once operative, would eventually embrace people of all races, all colors and all religions; there would be peace and harmony, hence "heaven" here on earth. All problems and challenges would be settled without wars and strife. Love would reign supreme in the transformed hearts and minds of nations. Thus, the term "kingdom of heaven" connotes the supremacy of love among mankind.

LIGHT

The Aramaic word *NOOHRA* means "light," "enlightenment" and "understanding." In many passages of the Bible, the term "light" symbolically represents God, His word, or a true teaching. This is why the psalmist says, "thy word is a lamp to my feet and a light to my path." Psalm 119:105.

In the first chapter of the book of Genesis, by a reference to light, the author gives a scientific insight into creation. The third verse reads, "And Alaha said, let there be light and there was light. And Alaha saw that the light was beautiful. . . ." (Aramaic text). Thus on the first day of creation light appeared.

Evidently the author of Genesis was a prophet-scientist or prophet-physicist. Many of the Old Testament prophets did fulfill this dual role. The ancient writer knew, as we do today, that everything in the universe can be reduced to light because light is the essence of all matter. Modern science further tells us that matter is gravitationally trapped light or energy and that light is the very source of man's physical existence on earth. The Old Testament author came to these conclusions thousands of years ago. He also used the term "light" metaphorically to mean "enlightenment" and "innate knowledge." In other words, the author felt that all creation before its appearance into the world of matter had been endowed with inner light.

Light also means a clear teaching. Jesus referred to himself as "the light of the world," an expression which signified that his teaching was like the great luminary of the world, the sun. And even as the sun pours out life and light upon our planet, so does the teaching of Jesus "pour out" life and understanding to the hearts and minds of people everywhere. Jesus' statement, "I am the light of the world," may also be paraphrased, "My teaching enlightens the world of men." Man sees clearly when there is light, and where there is light, man need not falter.

Another powerful declaration spoken by Jesus is, "You are the light of the world." We have a responsibility to let love, justice, compassion, and goodness shine as a way of life to illumine the world. The light of God's truth always shines in every century and in all generations to reveal a happier, healthier way of life for all mankind. Again the man from Galilee said, ". . . . he who follows my teaching shall not walk in darkness (ignorance), but shall find for himself the light of life." John 8:12, Aramaic text.

THE NAME OF JESUS

And in the sixth month the angel Gabriel was sent from God unto a city of Galilee, named Nazareth . . . And the angel said unto her, Fear not, Mary: for thou hast found favour with God. And, behold, thou shalt conceive in thy womb, and bring forth a son, and shalt call his name JESUS. Luke 1:26, 30–31, KJV.

YSHUA is the Aramaic name of Jesus. This name was a very common one in biblical lands and times, and it is still widely used today. The name "Jesus" (or Joshua) means "Savior," Deliverer," "Liberator" and "Rescuer." The popularity of the name was due to the people's veneration of Israel's courageous national hero and leader, Joshua. Under the skillful leadership of Joshua the twelve tribes of Israel were settled in the land of Canaan. It was he who led the conquest of Palestine.

The Aramaic name of Jesus—*YSHUA*— comes from the word *YASHUA*, and though the two words are spelled alike in Semitic letters, the Aramaic word is pronounced *ESHOA.*

According to the New Testament writers, Jesus had fulfilled many messianic prophecies. This is the reason Mary and Joseph were instructed in a dream to name their child "Savior" or "Joshua" because his mission was to save his people from their sins (errors). "And she shall bring forth a son, and thou shalt call his name Jesus: For he shall save his people from their sins." Matt. 1:21, KJV. The word "sin," *KHATA*, in Aramaic means "to miss the mark," and the word "save," *KHAIWAY* means "to revive," "to restore," "to give life" and "to resuscitate."

Jesus, through his life and teachings, was to revive and restore spiritual vitality to the hearts and minds of his people who were missing the mark and who had lost their way. Not only was he the hope for his nation, but also for all nations. This is why the angels sang at his birth, "Song and praise be to God in the highest, and throughout the earth peace and good hope for mankind." Luke 2:14, Aramaic text.

The term "Christ" is a title, not a name, and it comes from the Greek word *KRISTOS*, which was derived from the Aramaic language. The Aramaic word *M'SHEKHA* has three basic meanings: "the anointed," "the ordained," and "the consecrated" or "one who bears the light of God." All kings, priests and prophets were ordained to their respective offices with anointing oil, and kings also had the title of *M'SHEKHA*—the Anointed or Christ. Jesus of Nazareth was the Anointed or the Christ because his ordination was bestowed by Life, by the Living God, and not by any organization.

THE ONLY BEGOTTEN

And the Word was made flesh, and dwelt among us, (and we beheld his glory, the glory as of the only begotten of the Father,) full of grace and truth. John 1:14, KJV.

What did John mean by the expression "only begotten?" This term "begotten," is greatly misunderstood since biblical writers often express spiritual ideas and truths in human terms. God is the eternal Spirit. God never begets nor is He begotten. He is not subject to conditions of time, space, or birth. Nonetheless, Easterners speak of God as having ears, hands, eyes and even wings.

"Begotten"—*YEKHEDAYA*—in Aramaic also means "sole," "only," as well as "only begotten." The word implies "a sole heir," or "only son," and therefore it suggests "the beloved one," "precious one" or "the firstborn son" of the household. Among Aramaic-speaking people, the term is understood literally only when reference is made to fathers and sons, but when referring to God it is understood figuratively.

In the East the firstborn son becomes the "sole heir" of all the father owns. The firstborn is the glory and honor of his father and is the one who will succeed his father, carry his name, and inherit his business. He will also be in charge of all his father's servants and will give orders to his father's wives.

The term "only" in this Bible reference is used to mean that only Jesus at that time was openly and boldly declaring God as the Father of all people. His life was a vital demonstration of divine sonship. Therefore, Jesus became known as the "only son' of this universal and spiritual truth. The apostle Paul also states that Jesus is "the firstborn among many brethren." (See Rom. 8:29). Jesus constantly demonstrated his sonship by his good works, healings and his inexplicable resurrection from the dead. "And who came to be known as the Son of God with power and with the Holy Spirit, because he arose from the dead, and he is Jesus Christ our Lord." Rom. 1:4, Aramaic text. All people come to understand that they are sons of the living God through the teachings of the living Christ.

As an "only son" brings joy to the hearts of his parents and glorifies them, so does Jesus through his life and gospel bring joy to mankind. Man had lost the concept of his divinity, and Jesus reinstated man's awareness of having been created in God's image. For the Hebrew Scriptures declare that man is the image and likeness of God (See Gen. 1:26–27).

An Eastern father glories when he sees his only son because he sees himself recreated in his offspring. This is what is meant by the expression, "the glory as of the only begotten of the Father." According to the apostle John, it is only through the teaching of Jesus, the living Christ, that people learn of their divine sonship again and become children of the living God. "But those who received him, to them he gave power to become sons of God, especially to those who believed in his name." John 1:12, Lamsa translation. The word "power," *SHULTANA*, means "right" or "authority." The Aramaic expression "believe in his name" signifies "to believe in his teaching." Again in 1 John 3:2, "My beloved, NOW we are the sons of God . . ."

SYMBOLISM

And Jesus, when he was baptized, went up straightway out of the water: and, lo, the heavens were opened unto him, and he saw the Spirit of God

descending like a dove, and lighting upon him.
Matt. 3:16, KJV.

The phrase, "the heavens were opened," is an Eastern
way of saying that the universe rejoiced at the presence of
Jesus. It is through his teaching that the chasm which sepa-
rates heaven and earth in our minds is removed. The phrase
also means heaven was ready to welcome Jesus' mission.

"Dove" is used by biblical writers to indicate meekness
and purity. The dove was the first domesticated bird. When
Noah sent the dove out of the ark, it returned to him with a
blossomed twig from an olive tree. This was symbolic of
peace, harmony and tranquility. The flood was over and a
peaceful era was ahead.

In the Near East, the dove often makes its habitation
with man. It makes its nest in temples and church build-
ings and houses. The dove, because of its purity and
harmlessness, has won the hearts of people and therefore is
seldom molested. In the Near East when a pious and gentle
man is described, it is often said, "He is so good and
harmless that even a dove will sit on him." It is also said,
"He is so meek that a bird will not fly away from him."
Jesus also instructed his disciples to be "harmless as
doves," that is, to be pure, innocent and sincere so that
strangers would welcome them.

Spirit has neither shape nor form, but it is symbolized by
the biblical writers so that people may understand. The
Spirit of the Lord came upon Jesus as a pure, meek and
harmless bird; that is, a dove. This means that Jesus was received by God. John saw the Spirit while in a moment of
trance, exactly the way Ezekiel and other Hebrew prophets
had seen their visions of God and His Habitation.

The Dove was the sign of a new order of peace and understanding which was to replace the old order of fear and war.
Jesus was ready to embark on a new mission which was to
change the world and bring the nations to God. His visit to
the river Jordan met with the divine approval of his Father.

CHILD OF HELL

> Woe unto you, scribes and Pharisees, hypocrites! for
> ye compass sea and land to make one proselyte, and
> when he is made, ye make him twofold more the
> child of hell than yourselves. Matt. 23:15, KJV.

Terms of speech such as "child of hell" or "son of hell"
are prevalent in biblical lands. One often hears an individual say to another, "you child of wickedness." This means,
"Your actions are treacherous." *BAR-GAYHANNA*, son of
hell, means "a corrupt person good for nothing except to be
burned." According to Eastern customs, a tree which does
not bear fruit is good only for one thing—to be burned as
fuel.

The Pharisees travelled over land and sea in search of
converts. When a man converted to the new religion he usually became worse than he had been before. This is because
as a pagan he was unaware of the many evils which were invented by the religious educators who had converted him.
The Pharisees knew how to deceive people through their
false piety, how to cheat widows and orphans and exact
tithes of even the smallest herbs planted in the people's
gardens, such as dill and cumin. They did not teach the
important matters of the law such as mercy, justice, and
forgiveness. The converts learned the unjust habits of their
teachers and became more corrupt than their religious
guides; hence the meaning of the expression, "twofold
more the child of hell."

SATAN—A COMMON EXPRESSION

As Westerners, one of our main difficulties in the study
of the Bible is the fact that we take everything so literally.
Let us consider John 6:70 as an example. The traditional
translation reads: "Jesus answered them, Have not I chosen

you twelve, and one of you is a devil?'' The Eastern Aramaic text, however, changes very slightly. It reads, ''Jesus said to them, Did I not choose you, the twelve, and yet among you one is a Satan?''

The Aramaic term *SATANA*, ''Satan,'' is derived from the word *SATA*, and means ''to slip,'' ''to slide,'' ''to deceive,'' ''to miss the mark,'' and ''to cause one to be misled or go astray.'' A person who is called ''Satan'' is one who misses the mark or who has gone astray. ''Satan'' can also mean a misleading statement. The word ''Satan'' is a Babylonian-Aramaic term and was rarely used in the law of Moses and the prophets. It gradually crept into Jewish literature during the exile and post-exile period of Hebrew history.

On another occasion when Peter rebuked Jesus and tried to persuade him not to speak about his coming crucifixion and death, Jesus responded to Peter in a rebuke by calling him ''Satan''. ''Get behind me, Satan; you are a stumbling block to me; for you are not thinking of the things of God but of men.'' Matt. 16:23, Aramaic text.

The term ''Satan'' refers to Peter's misguided intention. The apostle attempted to redirect Jesus' course; hence to make his master miss the mark and not fulfill his destiny. Peter did it ignorantly; nonetheless, it still was misleading.

Now in the passage of Scripture referred to above, Jesus knew that among the twelve apostles one was a ''Satan.'' Judas, of course, was the one to whom Jesus referred. From the beginning of Jesus' ministry, Judas was a believer in Jesus, but when he realized that the prophet from Nazareth was not the militant political leader whom he and the people had anticipated, Judas attempted to disassociate himself from Jesus. Judas, feeling disillusioned, deserted the ranks of the apostles and betrayed his Lord and teacher.

However, when Jesus referred to Judas as ''Satan'' in this particular passage, he meant simply that Judas was insincere and deceptive. Such statements are common in Aramaic and Arabic speech, as one often hears people say to one another, *"SATANA,"* (you Satan). In colloquial speech *SATANA* also mean "an ingenious man," while in Arabic *SHYTAN* means "you devil." Thus, the terms from which our word "Satan" is derived do not refer to any malevolent, supernatural being, but are common expressions which refer to man's misbehavior.

Figurative Speech

> Verily, verily, I say unto you, If a man keep my saying, he shall never see death. Then said the Jews unto him, Now we know that thou hast a devil. Abraham is dead, and the prophets; and thou sayest, If a man keep my saying, he shall never taste of death. John 8:51–52, KJV.

According to what the elders of Israel taught during the time of Jesus, death was the end. Abraham and the prophets had died and were in their graves. It was the people's belief in death that made it a finality in their minds.

On another occasion Jesus had told them that God was the God of the living and not of the dead. "But as touching the resurrection of the dead, have ye not read that which was spoken unto you by God, saying, I am the God of Abraham, and the God of Isaac, and the God of Jacob? God is not the God of the dead, but of the living." Matt. 22:31–32, KJV. All Hebrew prophets and men of God were spiritually alive, but the people at that time did not realize this truth. According to Jesus' teaching, men of good deeds were to live through their good works and would never be forgotten.

Jesus on another occasion had instructed his disciples that some of them would never "taste death." In other words, the apostles' fame and teachings would be told from one generation to another. They would become immortal. Today the names of the prophets and apostles are read in more than eleven hundred languages.

The term "devil" in this instance means "a wild man," "an insane man," "a mentally disturbed person." The use of the term "devil" was acquired during the Jewish exile in Babylon. The Aramaic text reads, "The Jews said to him, now we are sure that you are insane. . ."

In the Near East all forms of insanity and mental disturbances are attributed to devils, demons and jinns. Medical terms as we use them today were unknown and are still unknown in many areas of the Near East. Psychological terms for mental illness and emotional problems were alien to Eastern minds.

Jesus was called insane because those who heard him were shocked by his promise of not "tasting death." It sounded ridiculous to them. How could they believe that this peasant from Nazareth was greater than their forefather Abraham, or even greater than the prophets?

LITTLE CHILDREN

Little children, yet a little while I am with you. Ye shall seek me: and as I said unto the Jews, Whither I go, ye cannot come; so now I say to you." John 13:33, KJV.

The Aramaic phrase, "little children," or "my sons," was used to convey the teacher's love for and closeness to his disciples.

In the Near East an ecclesiastical authority when addressing a letter to the members of his church will write, "My beloved sons." One also hears people engaged in conversation calling one another, "my father" or "my son." The elder usually addresses the younger as "my son."

Interestingly, according to the Eastern custom, unlearned men, no matter how old they are, may be called or addressed as "little children." When God called Jeremiah to preach to the people, Jeremiah said "I am a child." This means

"I am unlearned." In Arabic such persons are called *JAHIL*, "inexperienced."

PAUL TEACHES CRUCIFIXION

> I am crucified with Christ; nevertheless I live; yet not I, but Christ liveth in me; and the life which I now live in the flesh I live by the faith of the Son of God, who loved me, and gave himself for me. I do not frustrate the grace of God; for if righteousness come by the law, then Christ is dead in vain. Gal. 2:20–21, KJV.

"I am crucified with Christ," of course, is not to be taken literally. Many people construe this verse to mean that the life of the true follower of Christ *must* be one of suffering and poverty. But this was not the apostle's intended meaning. What he was saying was: I am sharing the same sufferings which Jesus endured on the cross, because I am living according to his way of life. In other words, Paul was being defamed, harassed and persecuted for the sake of the gospel of his Lord. Just as Jesus paid a great price, his own life, for his controversial teaching, Paul was doing the same by exposing himself to many dangers and hardships while preaching this new gospel.

The apostle understood the depth and meaning of the crucifixion; therefore he was able to surrender his life completely to God and to follow the teachings of the Christ. All worldly passions and aspirations weighed nothing in the balance, because Jesus Christ was all in all to him. The life Paul was now living was totally directed and motivated by the faith, i.e., the new understanding that Jesus brought to the Hebrew Scriptures, a faith which involved spiritual principles that were contrary to the principles of the world.

When the apostle says he does not "frustrate the grace of God," this is also to be understood as a figure of speech.

Paul knew that works of this law did not bring true righteousness. Rather, the grace of God revealed true righteousness. The law was originally given to help man, to direct him in life, not to crush his spirit or enslave him. When the law of Moses was broken, it brought condemnation and punishment, while the grace of God always brings love and forgiveness. "Because the law was given by Moses; but truth and loving kindness (grace) came by Jesus the Anointed." John 1:17, Aramaic text.

Victory Over Death

O death, where is thy sting? O grave, where is thy victory? The sting of death is sin and the strength of sin is the law. But thanks be to God, which giveth us the victory through our Lord Jesus Christ. 1 Cor. 15:55–57, KJV.

The word "death" in the Aramaic language means "to be present somewhere else." It does not mean total annihilation, nor does it mean to cease to exist. Death is not a finality.

Death is not and never has been man's enemy. Humanity through fear and misunderstanding has often interpreted death as a sinister and awesome opponent of life. The law of death which operates in all of nature keeps a balance in nature. This law is beneficial to the whole creation. Can you imagine what it would be like if all people since the beginning of mankind were still living on the earth in their fleshly bodies? It is the physical part of man which must return to the earth so that others may have their part in the drama of life. Man in his spiritual nature is in the image and likeness of God and is indestructible and eternal.

Death, where is your sting? Sheol, where is your victory? The sting of death is sin and the power of sin is the law. But thanks be to God who has given to us the victory through our Lord Jesus the Anointed One. 1 Cor. 15:55–57, Aramaic text.

Paul, as quoted above in his pastoral letter to the Corinthians, explains why death has a sting and why Sheol (a place where, according to Hebrew beliefs of that time, departed souls went to rest) has a victory over men. According to Paul's interpretation, man became "sin conscious" when the law of Moses was revealed, for the law reinforced the apparent power of sin by declaring what was right or wrong, clean or unclean. The result was that man often felt powerless over sin, sickness and death.

However, Jesus, through his own death and resurrection, destroyed the "sting" of death—sin. Through the teachings of Jesus man learned that sin (error, missing the mark) is forgivable and that individuals have power over their mistakes. The cross, to Semitic people, represented death. But through Jesus the cross came to represent new life, showing that mankind, through embodying a consciousness of the Christ, has authority over sin, sickness and death.

Jesus' dramatic and triumphant resurrection from the dark and dreaded grave was not an attempt to prove a religious doctrine of eternal life, but was intended to uncover a long-held secret of nature: that no life ever comes to an end. The resurrection clearly reveals life is spiritual in its essence and therefore eternal and not ephemeral.

Again the apostle Paul assures his disciple Timothy, ". . . And is now made manifest by the appearance of our Savior Jesus Christ, who has abolished death and has revealed life and immortality through the gospel." 2 Tim. 1:10. Jesus has destroyed the *fear* of death, not the process of death itself. It is the law of life that brings us into this world and it is the same law of life that carries us out.

It can be said that birth and death are the opposite extremes of the same rod. It is the power of death and decay that makes a freshly planted seed give birth to new life. The law of death causes life to continue and multiply.

During the last Passover meal that Jesus and his apostles shared together, he endeavored to encourage them. They were very depressed, gloomy and fearful because of the bleak and forboding future they were facing. Their hope of the political restoration of the Davidic kingdom and an all-conquering militant Messiah was fading away. Now the apostles' hearts were heavy with the thoughts of their beloved teacher's death.

Jesus said to them, "I will not leave you bereaved, I will come to you after a little while. And the world will not see me, but you will see me; because I live, you shall live also. In that day you will know that I am with my Father and you are with me, and I am with you." John 14:18-20, Aramaic text. After Jesus had been crucified and raised from the dead, he told his disciples, "Lo, I am with you always, to the end of the world." He will always reveal himself to his disciples. "He who has my commandments with him and obeys them is the one who loves me; he who loves me will be loved by my Father, and I will love and *reveal* myself to him." John 14:21, Aramaic text.

CONCLUSION

In this volume we have covered a great many subjects. But we have "caught" only a small glimpse of the powerful light that shines from Aramaic, the language of Jesus. In the volumes which are to follow, we will uncover even more precious treasures through the eyes of the Near East and unlock many new doors with the seven keys . . . Until then: Shlamay ookhubey dalaha awoon: elalam, allmeen . . . Peace and love from Alaha (God) our Father forever and ever.

Reference Notes

INTRODUCTION

1. Abraham H. Rihbany, *The Syrian Christ*, p. vi.
2. Daily American Newspaper, Rome, July 10, 1971.
3. See Philip K. Hitti, *The Near East in History*, The Aramaic Language.
4. See C. F. Burney, *The Aramaic Origin of the Fourth Gospel*; also, Charles Cutler Torrey, *The Four Gospels*, A New Translation, pp. 235–286, The Origin of the Gospels; also, Matthew Black, *Aramaic Approach to the Gospels and Acts*.
5. W. A. Wigram, *The Assyrians and Their Neighbors*, pp. 177,181.

CHAPTER 1

1. Allan Tarshish, *Not by Power*, p. 15.
2. New Standard Jewish Encyclopedia, 1970, pp. 139–140.
3. Newsweek, August 30, 1982, p. 73
4. George M. Lamsa, *The Book of Psalms*, p. xiv.
5. The Writings of Ishodad, translated by the author.

CHAPTER 2

1. George M. Lamsa, *Old Testament Light*, p. 56.
2. Ibid., pp. 96–97.
3. Ibid., pp. 600–602
4. Ibid., p. 620.
5. Ibid., p. 648.
6. George M. Lamsa, *New Testament Commentary*, pp. 315–316.
7. Ibid., p. 406.
8. George M. Lamsa, *More Light on the Gospel*, p. 202.

CHAPTER 3

1. The Writings of Mar Narsai, translated by author.
2. George M. Lamsa, *Old Testament Light*, pp. 901–907.
3. Ibid., pp. 793–795.
4. Abraham M. Rihbany, *The Syrian Christ*, pp. 12–13.
5. Ibid., pp. 12–13
6. Ibid., p. 25.
7. Ibid., p. 20.
8. George M. Lamsa, *More Light on the Gospel*, p. 90.

CHAPTER 4

1. W. A. Wigram, *The Assyrians and their Neighbors*, pp. 179, 185–186.
2. Abraham M. Rihbany, *The Syrian Christ*, p. 191.
3. Ibid., p. 191.
4. Ibid., p. 197.
5. Ibid., p. 28
6. Ibid., p. 127.
7. Ibid., pp. 148–149
8. Ibid., pp. 255–257.
9. George M. Lamsa, *Gospel Light*, pp. 317–320.
10. Abraham M. Rihbany, *The Syrian Christ*, pp. 64–65.
11. Ibid., p. 69.

CHAPTER 5

1. Abraham M. Rihbany, *The Syrian Christ*, p. 128.
2. Ibid., pp. 107–113
3. Ibid., pp. 316–317.
4. Ibid., pp. 316–317.
5. George M. Lamsa, *Gospel Light*, p. 38.
6. Ibid., p. 39.
7. Ibid., p. 41.
8. Ibid., p. 41.
9. Ibid., p. 42.
10. Abraham M. Rihbany, *The Syrian Christ*, pp. 94–95.

CHAPTER 6

1. Abraham M. Rihbany, *The Syrian Christ*, p. 140.
2. Ibid., p. 140.
3. See Dr. J. H. Hertz, chief rabbi of the British Empire, addi-

tional notes from *The Pentateuch and Haftorash Commentaries,*
p. 196.
  4. George M. Lamsa, *Old Testament Light,* pp. 862–863.
  5. Abraham M. Rihbany, *The Syrian Christ,* p. 118.

CHAPTER 7

1. Abraham M. Rihbany, *The Syrian Christ,* pp. 115–117.

CHAPTER 8

1. George M. Lamsa, *Old Testament Light,* pp. 105–106.

Bibliography

Ancient Aramaic *New Testament and Psalms*, (Peshitta): ABS 1950.

Berry, George Ricker, The Interlinear literal translation of the *Hebrew Old Testament*: Genesis and Exodus, Chicago: Follett Pub. Co., 1959.

Black, Matthew, *Aramaic Approach to the Gospels and Acts*, Oxford: Clarendon Press, 1946, 2nd edit. 1954, 3rd edit. 1967.

Burkitt, F. Crawford, *Early Eastern Christianity*, St. Margarfet's Lectures 1904, The Syriac-Speaking Church, E. P. Dutton & Co., New York; 1904.

Burney, C. F. *The Aramaic Origin of the Fourth Gospel*, London: Oxford University Press, 1922.

Burton, Richard F., *Thousand Nights and A Night*, vol. 10, Terminal Essay, London: Burton Club for Private Members only, 1886.

Cohen, A., Soncino Books of the Bible, *Isaiah*, commentary by Dr. Israel W. Sloti, London: Novello and Company, 1972.

Durant, Will, *Our Oriental Heritage*, New York: Simon and Schuster, 1954.

Emhardt, W. C. and Lamsa, George M., *The Oldest Christian People*, New York: Macmillan Co., 1926.

Fitzmyer, Joseph A., *A Wandering Aramean*, A Collection of Aramaic Essays, Chico, California: Scholar Press, 1979.

Genesis Through Malachi, Aramaic-Peshitta text, London: The Whitefriars Press Ltd., 1954.

Gibson, Margaret Dunlop, *The Commentaries of Ishodad of Merv*, London: Cambridge University Press, 1911.

161

Heschel, Abraham J., *The Prophet: The Jewish Publication Society of America*, New York, Harper and Row, 1962.

Hitti, Philip K., *The Near East in History*, New York: D. Van Nostrand Co. 1960.

_____, *History of the Arabs*, London: Macmillan and Co. 1937.

_____, *Syria, A Short History*, New York, The Macmillan Co., 1959.

Lamsa, George M., *The Holy Bible from Ancient Eastern Manuscripts*, Philadelphia: A. J. Holman Co., 1957.

_____, *Old Testament Light*, Englewood Cliffs: Prentice Hall Inc. 1964.

_____, *Gospel Light*, Philadelphia: A. J. Holman Co., 1939.

_____, *New Testament Commentary*, Philadelphia: A. J. Holman Co., 1945.

_____, *More Light on the Gospel*, Garden City: Doubleday and Co., 1968.

_____, *The Book of Psalms*, according to the Eastern version, Philadelphia: A. J.Holman Co., 1939.

_____, *Key to Original Gospels*, Philadelphia: The John C. Winston Co., 1931.

_____, *New Testament Origin*, Chicago: Ziff Davis Pub. Co., 1947.

Mingana, D. Alphonsi, *Narsai*, in two volumes in Aramaic, Mosul: Goormachtigh, 1905.

Naville, Edouard, *Archaeology of the Old Testament—Was the Old Testament Written in Hebrew?*, Robert Scott, Roxburghe House, London, 1913.

O'Disho, *Marganitha*, Kerala, India: Mar Themotheus Memorial Printing, 1965.

Orlinsky, Harry M., *Understanding the Bible through History and Archaeology*: Jewish Publication Society, New York City, Ktav Publishers, 1972.

Plaut, W. Gunther, *The Torah*, Genesis, New York: Union of American Hebrew Congregations, 1974.

Price, Ira Maurice, *The Ancestry of Our English Bible*, An account of manuscripts, texts and versions of the Bible, New York: Harper and Brothers, 1956.

Rihbany, Abraham M., *The Syrian Christ*, Boston: Houghton Mifflin Co, 1916.

———, *The Hidden Treasure of Rasmola*, Boston: Houghton Mifflin Co., 1914.

Roth, Cecil and Wigoder, Geoffrey, Editors in chief, *The New Standard Jewish Encyclopeida*, Garden City: Doubleday and Co., 1970.

Silver, Daniel Jeremy, *A History of Judaism* (vol. 1): Basic Books, Inc. Pub. New York, 1974.

Stewart, John, *Nestorian Missionary Enterprise*, A Church on Fire, Edinburgh: T. & T. Clark, 1928.

Torrey, Charles Cutler, *The Four Gospels*, a new translation, New York: Harper and Brothers Pub., 1947

Wight, Fred H., *Manners and Customs of Bible Lands*, Chicago: Moody Press, 1953

Wigram, W. A., *The Assyrians and Their Neighbors*, London: G. Bell & Sons, 1929.

Würthwein, Ernst, *The Text of the Old Testament*, Grand Rapids, Michigan: Wm. B. Eerdman Publishing Co., 1979.

ABOUT THE AUTHOR

Rocco A. Errico, D.D., founder and president of the Noohra Foundation of Costa Mesa, California, is an ordained minister, lecturer, author, biblical authority, and educator. He is a dynamic speaker whose unique Near Eastern approach to the Scriptures has made him one of the most sought-after lecturers in the nation.

For ten years Dr. Errico was tutored intensively by, and traveled with, the late George M. Lamsa, Th.D., world renowned Assyrian biblical scholar, foremost authority on the Aramaic language, and translator of the *Holy Bible From Ancient Eastern Manuscripts.*

Dr. Errico was accredited by Dr. Lamsa to teach the ancient Eastern Aramaic branch of Biblical Studies. In addition, he holds an honorary doctorate from St. Ephrem's Institute, Sweden. He serves as Professor of Biblical Studies in schools of ministry for various denominations, and he is a regular feature writer for several religious publications. He has held advisory positions with many boards of ecumenical religious organizations.

Students, ministers, bible teachers, and all those who seek a greater understanding of the Bible find Dr. Errico's approach helpful, practical, and enlightening. He is able to bridge the gap between the ancient biblical writers and the modern Western mind with clarity and simplicity. He provides an awareness that is uncluttered by denominational dogma, creed, or theological implications, which is important to all readers of the Bible.

Dr. Errico's proficiency in Aramaic, the language of Jesus, his knowledge of the customs, idioms, psychology, symbolism and philosophy of the Semitic peoples, and his fresh approach to the teachings of the patriarchs, prophets, Jesus and his apostles, make the Bible and its characters come alive. He is a spellbinding storyteller gifted with superb timing and dramatic delivery. His directness, humor, and understanding captivate his audiences. He is in continual demand as a lecturer for colleges, civic groups, churches of all denominations, workshops, and seminars and for guest appearances on radio and television programs throughout the United States and Canada.

Under the auspices of the Noohra Foundation, Dr. Errico continues to lecture, teach, and expand this program worldwide.

Write the Noohra Foundation for a free catalog of Aramaic Bible translations, books and cassette tapes and a brochure of classes, retreats, and seminars. Those interested in scheduling Dr. Errico for a personal appearance may also write to the Noohra Foundation:

Noohra Foundation
720 Paularino Avenue, Suite 210
Costa Mesa, CA 92626
PH: (714) 754-4186